POWERFUL CHAKRA HEALING TECHNIQUES

A Beginner's Guide to Activating, Self-Balancing, and Unblocking Your Chakras. Create Everyday Rituals for Your Health and Positive Energy

Melissa Gomes

https://smartpa.ge/MelissaGomes

Table of Contents

Freebies!

I have a **special treat for you**! You can access exclusive bonuses I created specifically for my readers at the following link! The link will redirect you to a webpage containing all my books and bonuses for each book. Just select the book you have purchased and check the bonuses!

>> https://smartpa.ge/MelissaGomes<<

OR scan the QR Code with your phone's camera

Bonus 1: Free Workbook - Value 12.95$

This **workbook** will guide you with **specific questions** and give you all the space you need to write down the answers. Taking time for **self-reflection** is extremely valuable, especially when looking to develop new skills and **learn** new concepts. I highly suggest you *grab this complimentary workbook for yourself*, as it will help you gain clarity on your goals. Some authors like to sell the workbook, but I think giving it away for free is the perfect way to say **"thank you" to my readers**.

Bonus 2: Free Book - Value 12.95$

Grab a **free short book** with **22+ Techniques for Meditation**. The book will introduce you to a range of meditation practices you can use to help you develop your inner awareness, inner calm, and overall sense of well-being. You will also learn how to begin a meditation practice that works for you regardless of your schedule. These meditation techniques work for everyone, regardless of age or fitness level. Check it out at the link below!

Bonus 3: Free audiobook - Value 14.95$

If you love listening to audiobooks on the go or would enjoy a narration as you read along, I have great news for you. You can download the audiobook version of *my books* for **FREE** just by signing up for a FREE 30-day trial! You can find the audio versions of my books (depending on availability) at the following link.

Join my Review Team!

Are you an avid reader looking to have more insights into spirituality? Do you want to get free books in exchange for an honest review? You can do so by joining my Review Team! You will get priority access to my books before they are released. You only need to follow me on Booksprout, and you will get notified every time a new Review Copy is available for my latest release!

For all the Freebies, visit the following link:

>> https://smartpa.ge/MelissaGomes<<

OR scan the QR Code with your phone's camera.

I'm here because of you

When you're supporting an independent author,
you're supporting a dream. Please leave
an honest review by scanning
the QR code below and clicking on the "Leave a
Review" Button.

https://smartpa.ge/MelissaGomes

Chapter 1: An Overview of the Chakras

As you go about your day, you get affected by what is happening around you. You experience emotional and physical changes that affect your energy depending on what you went through. With this, your energy pools, called chakras, are balancing out your thoughts, emotions, and feelings.

If this energy is blocked, though, it hinders all these processes. As this energy powers your body and mind, it brings about poor health and mental instability when your chakras are unbalanced. To keep the chakras clean and healthy, you need to unblock them.

In this chapter, I'll introduce the chakra system and describe how it impacts your physical, emotional, mental, and spiritual well-being.

How Do Chakras Work?

The human energy field works outside and inside you. It has many layers, including your aura, which communicates with your chakras and physical body. Think of it as your home, an element of water. It connects your energy bodies with your physical body: your organs and tissues. It goes through layers in your body. When your energy flows freely, the physical connection is like other important systems in your body that keep your energy flowing to energy points. This event reflects the energy outside the physical body, known as the aura.

Inside the physical body are your energy pools, or what we call chakras. This energy body consists of seven main chakras that work together to help you experience a healthy life. Chakras are energy wheels that swirl, each spinning faster or slower than the others. Just as an oyster creates pearls, your chakras are designed to create spiritual qualities: courage, happiness, and awareness. When your chakras are spinning at their peak, you are at your most vibrant and self-aware. The system operates on the understanding that all your chakras are balanced when you are in your best and highest vibration.

Your energy moves between the layers of your aura and your chakras, which is why the aura has an electromagnetic field. Your aura surrounds your physical body, extends several feet outwards, and comprises many layers or sheaths. These layers make up your seven main chakras. An individual can also have more chakras that interact with their higher state of consciousness. These chakras can influence well-being or imbalance when blocked.

While energy moves beyond the physical body, it can block the seven main chakras that need to be unblocked. These chakras are often clogged with subconscious psychological issues, such as anxiety, stress, trauma, guilt, grief, anger, fear, stress, addictions, and sadness. As human beings, you experience many layers concerning these emotions. In a way, these emotions are protecting you. Being aware of your emotions allows you to celebrate and accept them, then release them with the power of forgiveness.

Your energy moves between your energy layers. Each chakra has a specific area of influence, either within your body or in the aura. Vibrations pass from your chakras to your aura to communicate with each other and vice versa. This connection helps with proper energy flow, harmony, and balance of all your systems. When you meditate, your chakras are activated, and you can tap into your higher mind for energy and messages. All your chakras work together to support your development.

Chakras can also capture the energy of the universe around you and turn it into your aura and body. The more broad and open your chakras are, the more energy streams through your body. When we connect with the energy within our chakras and use it to heal ourselves on all levels, it expands our awareness.

Feeling Your Chakras

Relax and clear your mind in a quiet place. Hold your hands one inch apart, palms facing each other, to connect with your energy. You may feel a constant flowing sensation that happens between your hands. You will be able to feel the warmth in your hands as you become more accustomed to your energy. Then, try separating your hands slightly as if stretching the energy out, and then put them closer and feel the energy build up in between. If you do not feel anything at first, don't worry. You can do this practice any time to get used to your energy. Remember to become open and focused on yourself while doing this exercise.

Once you are familiar with your outside energy, you can start to feel your chakras as you place your hands on where your main chakras are located. For example, your heart chakra is located at the center of your chest. As you feel your heartbeat and focus, you will also feel your energy expand. Once you are comfortable doing this exercise, you may close your eyes. You will feel the energy moving throughout your body. You may feel any sensations and emotions you may have trapped in your body.

Another example is from your throat chakra. You can feel your energy pool at the center of your neck, right on the thyroid gland. The third eye chakra, in addition, is located slightly above your eyebrows. Alternately, you may feel the energy pool somewhere on the feet and moving up to the chest. This will reflect how your airflow works—from your feet to your lungs. If you are open and clear, you may have a mental image that white energy is flowing through your body. As you practice this, you can develop your way of feeling them and become familiar with your energetic bodies.

These sensations may occur as emotions of grief, guilt, anger, or sadness. You may feel the energy moving through certain energy points in your body. Whether or not you have blockages in your chakras, you will feel the energy moving throughout your body. Feeling your chakras will allow you to get better acquainted with yourself. As you become more familiar, you will also feel the blockages in your chakras and how they influence your well-being. If you have trouble feeling your chakras or don't feel anything, you may try expanding your awareness beyond the physical sensation of feeling. With practice over time, this feeling of connectedness with your chakras and the energy center will deepen and start to feel more natural.

The Healing Power of Chakras

Ancient knowledge about chakras has been practiced for centuries by numerous ancient cultures. Their teachings were discovered by the Western world through the East and adapted and developed in modern times. The Eastern world is very knowledgeable about the physical and energetic body that connects to it because this region has been home to spiritualism and mysticism for thousands of years. The awakening of chakras began in the 1900s with the teachings of individuals who separated different chakras. Western science is currently discovering that there is energy and power behind chakras and proves there are healing benefits that have yet to be discovered.

The Eastern world naturally becomes aware of energy and its movements through their daily life. Hence, their perception of energy is similar to how energy flows in the human body. Their wisdom has existed for thousands of years and is not discovered with modern science. Their knowledge about the human body and their philosophy about how energy and all natural things have distinct vibrations allow them to create advanced practices for self-healing and spiritual growth.

Our lives are completely in harmony, and our health is optimal when our chakras are in balance. On the other hand, when a chakra becomes blocked, we eventually experience emotional distress or disease.

The Chakra Healing Myths

Here are some widely known myths about chakras and how they are proven untrue:

- **Myth 1: Chakra healing can only be done by professionals.** On the contrary, chakra healing is an internal process, not an external one. While healers can assist you on your path, you are ultimately in charge of your recovery. Practitioners guide you on how to heal yourself, but whether or not you will allow healing to take place is up to you.

- **Myth 2: A particular religion is associated with chakra healing.** People from all walks of life are now practicing chakra healing.Numerous religions and spiritual paths have embraced the teachings and techniques behind chakra healing because they honor the natural flow of energy.

- **Myth 3: Chakra healing is an umbrella term for energy healing.** Energy healing does include chakra healing, but it is not the only healing practice. Energy healing methods are different. Chakra healing focuses on your individual well-being and integrates the spiritual journey of healing. People have understood that energy healing is an umbrella term for different practices, including shamanic healing, reiki, crystal healing, and other methods.

- **Myth 4: Chakra therapy is a dark or demonic ritual.** True healing of your chakras is to allow yourself to become highly aware and conscious. The goal is to increase your awareness to unclutter your chakras. Becoming a highly sensitive person is not evil or negative; it allows you to see through the illusions of life. As your awareness grows, emotionally and spiritually, you can acknowledge your blocks and heal yourself. Your chakras are your reflection and the key to becoming your highest self.

- **Myth 5: Chakra healing is only for rockstars and celebrities.** Famous people can possibly influence your decisions, but chakra healing is a journey of self-realization for everyone. Chakra healing is about learning who you truly are and tapping into your higher self. You are not affected by anything outside. Everything within you reflects how you deal with various experiences, thoughts, and feelings that you allow. The main benefit of chakra healing is finding out who you are and allowing you to be compassionate with yourself by knowing your real identity, not by who you think you should be based on societal norms.

Tips for Chakra Healing

Balancing your chakras can open new pathways and allow you to tap into your full potential. Opening up to your fears and sadness will help you become more conscious and aware every day of your life. This new balance allows you to experience life in a way you never have. Chakra healing allows you to align yourself with the source. This path is about living in the present moment and allowing your experiences to transform you.

Developing more awareness can lead you to realize where and how blockages occurred. As you start your chakra healing journey, here are a few pointers to help you get through it smoothly.

1. **Rushing is not healing.** Chakra healing takes time and cannot be "sped up." Be kind to yourself as you develop, and remember that everyone has a unique development process perfectly suited to them. Healing is like playing an instrument: you must practice constantly to get better. If you rush the healing process for a temporary solution, you will struggle to heal your chakras properly. If you need to take time for yourself to rebalance and heal, then do so. It is best for your overall well-being to allow the healing process to occur gently, evenly, and at your own pace. Everything is energy and vibrations; you can influence energy with your thoughts.

2. **Do your research.** As you try a new healing technique, please pay attention to your body and how it responds as it is healing with you. If something doesn't feel right, it is important to listen to your body's signals and understand what is happening. The "one shoe fits all" policy does not apply to healing methods; what works for one may not work for the other.

3. **Never force your energy or push yourself past what you are comfortable with.** When you are done with a certain part of the healing process, give yourself some time off to prepare for the next step. Healing does not happen overnight and can only become permanent with patience and consistency.

Chapter 2: Know your Kundalini Energy

Kundalini energy is the primal, enlightening force. It awakens all of your chakras, often around the same time. This awakening usually takes place around the middle stage of your life and shifts your life's purpose. Kundalini, or 'coiled' in Sanskrit, is symbolized by a snake coiled up at the base of the spine, the primordial energy force lying dormant or unable to extend into the rest of the body.

This event can happen on the secular level and the spiritual level. On the spiritual level, you can release your Kundalini from fear by performing mindfulness practices. Sometimes, the awakening is not brought on by physical means. Other times, it may be triggered by a traumatic event or major changes. You might not fix one's awareness of attachment, or you might be lucky, leading to the release of Kundalini energy without preparing for it.

If your Kundalini energy awakens spontaneously, it will more than likely awaken the energy center called the crown chakra, located on top of your head. If you believe the energy forces to be separated, the feeling could be likened to the top of your head exploding, leading to the opening and blossoming of the top of your head, causing it to become lighter. You might feel different: both hollow and, at the same time, wondering what just happened. You may also feel like you need to cry or laugh simultaneously; this is the release of all emotions at once. Kundalini's spiritual awakening is often accompanied by intense energy.

However, if you are not fully prepared for the intense awakening or if there are still blockages in your energy points, your

Kundalini energy can get stuck. This can cause many things that are physically uncomfortable to happen. In such a case, your Kundalini is stuck in either the sacral or the solar plexus chakra. Soon, one's lower chakras would be overstimulated without intervention or preparation, resulting in excessive sweating, a racing heartbeat, high blood pressure, insomnia, an upset stomach, and nausea. These symptoms normally occur before the lower chakras are awakened, and the energy forces cannot circulate properly through the body as they should. For these cases, I have written another book about Kundalini Awakening that will help you get through the overwhelming energy surge. This book teaches you to address the blockages and heal your chakras.

Identifying Chakra Points

Your main chakras control your physical and spiritual well-being. You can find out which chakras you are mainly functioning from by looking at the chakra points on the body and what to do when blockages take place.

The Root Chakra

The Root Chakra is located near the perineum and is the Kundalini energy center. This chakra governs everything from your sense of self to material wealth to survival instincts. It points to fear of abandonment or being rejected, fear of finances, and fear of aging and death.

When the root chakra is fully activated, you feel grounded, safe, and trust natural laws. One who lives in a state of harmony and positive affirmations can manifest all of their desires. You are perceived as intelligent, stable, and have a strong sense of spirituality. When your root chakra is balanced and open, you feel secure in your existence in the physical realm. You know you are a precious gift to the universe, and you believe there is no better place to be than here.

When the root chakra is out of harmony, you might feel insecure and anxious, and your material world suffers as a result. You can feel ungrounded and disconnected from Mother Earth. You may also have issues with tribal beliefs or family wounds, causing you to hold on to them and reject others. If these blockages are not dealt with, you might develop physical conditions such as sciatica and low back problems.

More Details about the Chakra

Name in Sanskrit: *Muladhara*

Chakra Color: Red

Element: Earth

Other Name References: Base chakra, the first chakra

Life Lesson: To feel secure in the physical plane, to feel safe within one's skin

Blockages

Causes: Guilt, fear of being alive

Cure: Practice forgiveness and acceptance of self

Blockage Manifestations

- **Physical:** Backache, sciatica and leg problems, lowered immunity, hemorrhoids, constipation, depression, weight issues

- **Mental:** Lack of ambition, lack of providing for family necessities, ability to stand up for self, lack of positive affirmations or motivation

- **Spiritual:** Feeling ungrounded, fear or hesitant to trust or open up to others

Items to Help Remove Blockages

Yoga Poses for the Root Chakra: Twist poses, Standing pose, Tree Pose, Warrior Pose, Wheel Pose, Bridge Pose, Standing Forward Bends

Crystals: Black Obsidian, Black Tourmaline, Red Jasper, Kyanite, Fire Agate, Black Moonstone, Smoky Quartz, Hematite, Bloodstone, and Garnet.

Essential Oils: Patchouli, myrrh, sandalwood, ginger

The Sacral Chakra

The sacral chakra is located in your pelvis, a couple of inches below the navel. It is also associated with money, creative capacity, and happiness. It governs your creative juices and sexuality. Both men and women have sacral chakras. Stimulating this chakra can help your sex life.

The sacral chakra is stimulated by sexual energy, which releases you from the cycle of birth and death. It awakens and fills us with vitality. When the sacral chakra is activated, you feel nurtured and loving. You are in the flow of your creative expression, feel at peace with your abundance, and are connected to the emotional aspects of intimate connections.

When blockages are present in the sacral chakra, you have difficulty expressing your feelings and are out of touch with pleasure. You may start holding unprocessed anger and feel limited in expressing your creativity. You may also have relationship issues, reproductive issues, or feel unstable around aspects of your sexuality. When this chakra is blocked, you might start having issues making loving decisions or experiencing passion. You may also be unable to set boundaries or assert yourself with your partner.

More Details about the Chakra

Name in Sanskrit: Svadhisthana

Chakra Color: Orange

Element: Water

Other Name References: Pelvic chakra, the second chakra, sacral plexus chakra

Life Lesson: To connect with others using emotions without losing your sense of self, to express creativity and sexuality freely and healthily

Blockages

Causes: Sexual abuse, sexual trauma, gender issues

Cure: Learn the law of attraction; set goals and affirmations; develop a spiritual foundation of being grounded and centered on achieving goals.

Blockage Manifestations for the Sacral Chakra

- **Physical:** Lower back pain, gynecological problems, pelvic pain, sexual dysfunctions, cellulite, uterine, bladder or kidney problems

- **Mental:** Emotional repression, self-criticism, instability around emotional matters, lack of sense of honor and power in relationships

- **Spiritual:** Aversion to sexuality, feeling stagnant, fear of expressing one's feelings, lack of creative expression, guilt relating to emotional issues

Items to Help Remove Blockages

Yoga Poses for the Sacral Chakra: Standing poses, Camel Pose, Warrior Pose, Bridge Pose, Wheel Pose, Locust Pose, Downward Dog Pose

Crystals: Carnelian, aventurine, amber, citrine, garnet, and jasper. **Essential Oils:** Rose, Jasmine, Frankincense, Geranium, Cypress, Neroli, Ylang Ylang, Geranium, and Tuberose.

The Solar Plexus Chakra

The Solar Plexus Chakra is located halfway between your navel and your chest. This chakra handles everything from self-esteem and self-love to calling your power into action through will, courage, and strength. This chakra stimulates your will to take action.

When the Solar Plexus Chakra is in harmony, you feel strong and can confidently make decisions. You enjoy good health and are passionate about getting what you want. You are physically healthy, mentally alert, and spiritually conscious. You feel whole and centered, know your self-worth, and have inner peace and calm. When you are detoxified, your energy can move freely through your system and keep you grounded. It allows you to experience your truth and thrive in your authenticity.

When this chakra is blocked, you feel tired and run down, even in physical solitude. The "I don't want" attitude takes over. You procrastinate making decisions, need to dominate and control, and may even manifest self-hatred. Blockages in this chakra might make you feel fearful or powerless. You can develop colon problems and other digestive issues if this is not dealt with. You might also suffer from depression or feelings of insecurity, especially if you are a victim of abuse or violence.

More Details about the Chakra

Name in Sanskrit: *Manipura*

Chakra Color: Yellow

Element: Fire

Other Name References: The third chakra, power chakra, core chakra

Life Lesson: To develop self-esteem, empower yourself, follow your life's path to the core of your beliefs

Blockages

Causes: Issues in control and power, hidden anger

Cure for solar plexus chakra: Set personal goals and take positive actions, take back your power

Blockage Manifestations

- **Physical:** Digestive problems, overweight, diabetes, gastric ulcers, liver dysfunction, fatigue, hepatitis

- **Mental:** Fear, lack of trust, intimidation, lack of self-respect or respect for others, lack of honor, irresponsibility

- **Spiritual:** Fear of change or taking action, lack of intuition, lack of direction or a sense of purpose

Items to Help Remove Blockages

Yoga Poses for the Solar Plexus Chakra: Warrior Pose, Cobra Pose, Wheel Pose, Warrior II Pose, Downward Dog Pose

Crystals: Citrine, Yellow Danburite, Carnelian, Yellow Selenite, Sunstone, Golden Quartz, Topaz

Essential Oils: -sandalwood, myrrh, Atlas cedarwood, Ylang ylang, lemongrass, helichrysum, lavender

The Heart Chakra

The heart chakra connects the physical and spiritual aspects of yourself and also your Higher Self. It is located at the chest or heart level and within your energy field. The heart chakra holds the ability to love and feel compassion. It gives you the ability to be in society and deal with others. It is the center of love, compassion, and all forms of giving and receiving.

The heart chakra is the center of compassion, kindness, empathy, and love. Love is a skill to learn, to perfect. Love keeps us open, sharing, and joyous. When you are open and free to love, you start taking responsibility for your feelings and actions. When the heart chakra is balanced, you will feel that you are part of a loving community and can love yourself and others unconditionally. You will begin feeling centered in who you are and connected to all life. You are connected with your Higher Self and interested in the spiritual lessons of life.

When the heart chakra is blocked, you feel lonely and isolated. You may experience feeling unworthy or unlovable. If your sense of your heart center is out of alignment, your physical heart may also be out of balance. You might start having palpitations, breathing problems, or pain in your chest. You may also experience depression or difficulty in forming healthy relationships. It can also cause difficulties in your financial and career life. When the energy is not flowing well, it might result in disconnection from others.

More Details about the Chakra

Name in Sanskrit: *Anahata*

Chakra Color: Green

Element: Air

Other Name References: The fourth chakra

Life Lesson: To love yourself unconditionally, to feel connected to all things, and that life loves you unconditionally

Blockages

Causes: Emotional trauma, issues around self-worth, feeling unlovable

Cure: Set your intentions to love, honor, and value yourself, to reconnect with the spiritual aspect of your heart

Blockage Manifestations

- **Physical:** Heart attack, high blood pressure, lung or breathing issues, allergies, asthma

- **Mental:** the need for opinion to be heard, becoming judgmental, fear, cynicism, suspicion, lack of compassion or empathy, hatred of self or others, self-defeatism

- **Spiritual:** Beliefs that prevent love, self-centeredness, lack of compassion or empathy, lack of trust in life

Items to Help Remove Blockages

Yoga Poses for the Heart Chakra: Forward Bends, Cobra Pose, Seated Forward Bend, Triangle Pose, Half Moon Pose, Cow Face Pose, Legs Up the Wall Pose, Wheel Pose

Crystals: Emerald, Aquamarine, Jade, Charoite, Fluorite, Chrysoprase, Apophyllite, Eudialyte, Peridot, Angelite

Essential Oils: Angelica Root, Geranium,

The Throat Chakra

The throat chakra has much to do with our true, authentic voice, where faith and understanding combine. It is located in the part of the throat above the larynx, just below the jaw. This chakra is essential for building connections with others and accepting that change is a necessary part of life.

When you align and activate the throat chakra, you connect to your truth, belief system, and true voice. This chakra is associated with the blue color. This chakra allows you to be expressive and communicate well when open and aligned. This is the voice of truth. It is the center of personal power and authority. You can confidently speak your truth when your throat chakra is open and balanced. You can share your beliefs and learn from others. You can gain the courage to express yourself diplomatically. Once you learn to express yourself well, your creativity and ability to communicate on all levels improve.

When the throat chakra is blocked, it may feel like you cannot express your true feelings, and expression becomes limited. You may become secretive or fearful of sharing. You may even find it difficult to communicate and be understood. You may have dry or sore throats. People with thyroid problems have difficulty feeling the throat chakra open and aligned, which tends to cause more emotional struggles in this area.

More Details about the Chakra

Name in Sanskrit: Vishuddha

Chakra Color: Blue

Element: Ether

Other Name References: The fifth chakra, the chakra of communication

Life Lesson: To speak truth eloquently, to feel free and authentic

Blockages

Causes: Perfectionism, unclear expression, blaming others for troubles, not listening to your heart

Cure: Express truth, listen to your heart's wisdom, stand in your power

Blockage Manifestations

- **Physical:** Allergies, issues around communication, vocal problems, issues in the neck or shoulders, thyroid problems, scoliosis, gum difficulties

- **Mental:** Lack of expression, rigid thinking patterns

- **Spiritual:** Not speaking enough, not listening to higher wisdom through your heart

Items to Help Remove Blockages

Yoga Poses for the Throat Chakra: Standing Forward Bends, Forward Folds

Crystals: Turquoise, Blue Lace Agate, Sodalite, Lapis Lazuli, Celestite

Essential Oils: Lavender, chamomile, peppermint, Bergamot, Geranium

The Third Eye Chakra

The Third Eye Chakra is found at the brow or eye level. It is our spiritual vision center. This chakra is the center of our psychic vision, the art of prophecy. It is the connection between you and the external world beyond your five senses. It lets you see your true purpose here on Earth and channels your natural intuitive abilities.

Once your third eye is balanced, you can initiate change within yourself. Your intuition is stronger, and you gain more inner knowledge. It helps you to see the bigger picture and know the correct path to follow in life. The third eye is your doorway to spiritual awakening. Once open and balanced, you can see beyond the physical realm into the mysteries of life. It is the core of your intuition. This chakra also allows you to observe lucid dreams and learn from the visions you experience. The third eye chakra helps you gather information from your environment and connects you to the spirit realm. It gives you the wisdom needed to weigh your thoughts and judgments. It is the center of choice and the ability to gather knowledge.

When the third chakra is blocked or out of balance, your ability to analyze, solve problems objectively, and make good decisions, becomes difficult. When your focus or attention is on the physical world, you might lose your ability to see into the spiritual world. This block can make you more fearful of the world around you. You could also lose the ability to be in touch with your spiritual side and tune with your inner guidance. In extreme cases, people with a blocked third eye chakra may be unable to concentrate, become paranoid, and develop extreme anxiety.

More Details about the Chakra

Name in Sanskrit: *Ajna*

Chakra Color: Indigo

Element: Light

Other Name References: The sixth chakra, brow chakra, forehead chakra

Life Lesson: To see and receive the truth, to be centered within yourself

Blockages

Causes: Worrying too much, being too critical, isolation, lack of trust in intuition

Cure: Meditation, reflection, journaling, trusting intuition

Blockage Manifestations

- **Physical:** Migraines, anxiety, spinal difficulties, stroke, neurological problems like brain tumors, vision impairment, deafness

- **Mental:** Issues in relationships, lack of trust, self-evaluation issues, feeling inadequate, emotional intelligence, inability to learn from experience

- **Spiritual:** Fear of the unknown, lack of self-acceptance, anger, fear

Items to Help Remove Blockages

Yoga Poses: Warrior Poses, Triangle Pose, Dolphin Pose

Crystals: Lapis Lazuli, Amethyst, Clear Quartz, Tanzanite, Lepidolite, Kyanite, Selenite, Fluorite, Mookaite

Essential Oils: Lavender, sandalwood, frankincense, Clary sage

The Crown Chakra

The crown chakra is located, as the name states, at the crown of the head. It connects you to the spiritual realm above. It is the center of your consciousness and will. Our connection to Divine Consciousness, our divine purpose, is at its peak when our crown chakra is open and balanced. It is the place where your inner self connects with outer divinity. When open and balanced, the crown chakra allows you to connect and communicate with the Divine Power. It can help you work through and release past karma from your life. It connects you with knowledge and wisdom beyond you by giving you access to larger universal knowledge.

When the crown chakra is balanced, you feel connected to the entire world and receive spiritual inspiration. You are more aware of the spiritual aspects of your life. You have vast knowledge and wisdom at your fingertips, understanding beyond the three-dimensional plane. You also feel more receptive to guidance from the universe. Patterns of restraint and compliance unfold before you, and you will realize that people are being programmed to become two-dimensional beings, whereas you are multi-dimensional. You feel connected to our ancestors, spiritual guides, and masters. You would start feeling that higher intelligence is guiding you around the universe. You live in the knowledge of Unity, which means you are connected to the Divine and can elevate your consciousness.

When the crown chakra is blocked or damaged, you may feel disconnected from your spirit. You may crave spiritual guidance but may think you are ignored or punished. You may feel drained of energy for no apparent reason. Your sixth sense and intuition may become blocked and make it difficult to make decisions. You may lose interest in your surroundings and start losing inspiration and creativity, ultimately becoming disconnected from your Highest Self.

More Details about the Chakra

Name in Sanskrit: *Sahasrara*

Chakra Color: Purple, White, Gold

Element: Ether, Thought

Other Name References: Seventh chakra, head chakra

Life Lesson: To accept your divine purpose and honor your spirituality

Blockages

Causes: Unresolved anger or lack of trust in the Divine Power or Highest Self

Cure: Meditation, relaxation, reflection, prayer

Blockage Manifestations

- **Physical:** Depression, anxiety, fatigue without physical causes, apathy, high sensory sensitivity, alienation

- **Mental:** Confusion, indecision, and lack of follow-through

- **Spiritual:** Lack of spiritual connection

Items to Help Remove Blockages

Yoga Poses: Goddess Pose, Happy Baby Pose, Warrior Pose

Crystals: Amethyst, Herkimer Diamond, Selenite, Moonstone, Labradorite, White Topaz, Kunzite, Moldavite

Essential Oils: Peppermint, lotus, frankincense, sage, sandalwood

Chapter 3: Opening your Chakras

This chapter will discuss how to harness chakra power and other ways to maintain a balanced chakra system. In extreme cases, receiving acupuncture or Reiki treatment will greatly help balance one's chakras. Positive visualization, exercise, and a balanced diet are a few steps to maintaining a healthy body and aura.

Many individuals and therapists are unfamiliar with the concept of chakras which are energy centers in the human energy field. Most of us are unaware of their existence and tendencies to be imbalanced in our physical, spiritual, or emotional lives. Only recently, the Western healing arts began to acknowledge the chakra system and the longstanding imbalance of our physical, emotional, and spiritual health. The Eastern view sees health as an issue of the spiritual body. The Eastern view believes that we are made up of three bodies, or the three-part soul, and our physical bodies reflect our spiritual, emotional, and mental bodies.

As the physical body is the most material part of you, its alignment or balance with the other materials is important to maintain your physical health. An unbalanced physical body can lead to an imbalance in our emotional bodies, which affects our spiritual bodies. And so, the mind-body connection becomes a cycle by taking care of your physical body and spiritual energy.

In Western societies, our view of health is centered on the physical body. We are taught from a young age that illness is carried in physical objects and passed through our skin. With advancements in today's science, we understand more about the body and the immune system's ability to fight infection and disease. Western medicine has a successful track record in treating physical ailments.

When researching human vibrational therapy, I could not help but become aware of the human chakra system and how the imbalance of your system can affect you. To fully understand what chakra energy is all about, I went back to my roots to look at what the ancient healing arts had to say about the human body and the energy field.

Harnessing your Energy Pools

You can use several methods at home to help heal your chakras, including visualizations and meditations, changing old habits, practicing yoga, using crystals and essential oils, and getting the most out of your food. You can also use binaural music, visualization, crystals, or breaking old habits to help relieve your energy blockages to energize your chakra. As you have started to explore your seven chakras and their physical location in the body in the previous chapter, it noted that each chakra has a different location and function in how it manifests on your body. In this chapter, you will learn how to harness the power of each of your seven chakras by balancing them regularly. Here are a few methods to achieve a balanced chakra system. The methods discussed in this chapter can be used in combination with each other or separately.

Meditation and Visualization

Meditation can help you calm your mind, improve your mental clarity, promote emotional positivity, deep knowing, and concentration, and ground you when you feel scattered. It can also help you connect with your chakras, strengthen them and release emotional baggage and tension.

Visualization is another method that works like meditation. You can use actual images or images in your mind that will create peace within yourself while tuning into your energies and chakras. This method is often practiced by people who want to manifest something in their life. Visualizing, however, requires that you are focused and motivated to see results, as with meditation.

Other methods of meditation that you may find effective are quiet time by yourself to listen to music or the sounds of nature. You can walk by yourself and observe nature and the animals around you as you clear your mind of external thoughts. You can also listen to guided meditation. This style of meditation uses rhythmic or classical music with a strong beat and different tones to stimulate your chakras as you relax your mind.

Modern medicine now acknowledges visualization or meditation to affect one's mindset positively. Research has shown that meditation can help lower blood pressure levels,anxiety and prevent cancer. Visualization releases stress and promotes overall well-being, allowing your body and mind to relax and heal from within. You could practice healing meditations by imagining a white light glowing from your heart center as you visualize your chakras opening. This method can be done at any time of the day and is not limited by time, condition, season, or place. Here is a simple visualization practice for you:

- Visualize the light filling your chakras and connect your energy body with the white light.

- Once you visualize your chakras as vibrant, relaxed, and glowing, you can release any negative thoughts or emotions that are blocking your chakras.

Visualization is the practice of taming your thoughts by visualizing something positive and inspiring to you while imagining the positive outcome of your intentions. For example, suppose you want to heal yourself of an illness. In that case, you can heal your physical ailments by visualizing yourself as being healthy and the positive outcome of curing your illness while visualizing that you love yourself and deserve to get better.

There are countless methods to practice visualization and meditation, and most don't require you to be still for 5 to 10 minutes. Still, most involve following your breathing pattern, relaxing and focusing your mind on one thing, fully releasing thoughts and emotions, creating inner peace within yourself, and channeling positive energies. Meditation methods can be as simple as sitting in a quiet spot, closing your eyes, and focusing on your breath for a few minutes. Use essential oils or crystals to help calm yourself and ground your energy for a more therapeutic meditation.

Meditation is a practice that has been time-tested throughout the ages and is not just a trend. It can reduce physiological symptoms of anger in both seasoned and novice meditators. You can use these methods to calm your mind and refocus your energy, and it will all tie in and strengthen your energy centers and chakras. You can also visualize or imagine your chakras while you are practicing meditation. Sit in a meditative pose and focus your mind on a specific chakra if you wish. Here is a simple meditation method:

- Sit with your legs crossed, eyes closed, hands resting in your lap, or whichever position you prefer, and say or think the word "peace."

- Imagine that you are breathing in peace and out the anxiousness, anger, or negative energy you are holding within yourself or experiencing in your life.

Meditation is an exercise that alludes to your mind to let go of thoughts for a brief moment and tap into your spiritual connection. It helps you release negative thoughts that keep you from achieving your full potential by cluttering your mind. Remember that the energy you release while meditating is a very powerful energy source that can affect yourself and your surrounding environment.

Meditation can be done anywhere, anytime, and it helps us shift into higher consciousness, create mindfulness, and extend peace into the rest of our lives. Meditation takes you beyond your thoughts to the deeper silence within you. Meditation is a practice you do for yourself and it is a wonderful way to give yourself some much-needed rest throughout the day. You do not have to sit in silence to meditate. You can also pair your meditation with binaural music to help you focus on your breathing.

Binaural Music

Binaural music is in the form of meditation music or certain sounds of nature mixed or synthesized together, produced in waves measured in hertz. It is a music mix that profoundly affects your brain by using binaural beats to stimulate your brain into producing relaxing hormones such as oxytocin and serotonin. The mix floods your brain through each ear with slightly different beats and frequencies. The left and right hemispheres of your brain will then produce slightly different pulses or beats that work in tandem with one another to create a synchronized state. This helps you meditate as it helps you enter a meditative state easily. Beats produced through this method can help you focus on a specific aspect and help you with chakra healing and, ultimately, in achieving spiritual awakening.

You can try using binaural beats or listening to the chakra track of your choice to help you heal and balance your chakras, heal your body from a certain illness, reduce stress and depression, or reach a higher state of consciousness. These chakra tracks are a subliminal way to condition your mind and body to new thinking patterns and help you break old habits.

Breaking Old Habits

The first step to breaking old habits is creating awareness around the bad habit or issue that we are holding in a specific chakra. Once we are aware of the problem behavior or bad habit, we can then work to change that behavior. You can choose from one of several methods with binaural beats to help you break old patterns in your life as you bring about positive transformation and reactions from your body and chakras.

Chakras control your emotions and thoughts and connect to your body through different channels. You will feel good and healthy when your chakras are balanced and aligned. You can heal your chakra channels by breaking old habits like changing the way you think about things, where you put your attention, how you think and feel about yourself, and how you act and react to people or situations. These methods will help you heal your chakras and balance them to improve your well-being and energy.

Crystals

Working with crystals and stones helps us engage with the natural Earth energy, heal, and elevate consciousness. They are natural sources of healing energies that exist in a space with their vibrations. These vibrations match our conscious thoughts, feelings, and emotions. They can ultimately affect our physical well-being and produce various reactions within our physical being. Using a stone or crystal includes its specific color, texture, and healing properties to help balance your chakras.

There are many ways to work with crystals, including carrying a small crystal on your person, placing chakra-specific crystals on their particular chakra, or simply holding a crystal in your hands during meditation. Our hands are well-known energy pathways, and you can absorb their positive energies by cradling a stone in your hands. Crystals and stones are energy conduits and can bring out different reactions based on how we hold and work with them. You can place crystals on or around your chakras for proper alignment and flow as well as optimal well-being.

You can now find shops with a jewelry line that offers natural stones, crystals, and stones of healing properties as embellishments. These are great accessories to adorn your body while healing, channeling positive energy throughout the day, or meditating to release negative energy and elevate your positivity. You can wear or hold specific stones while you meditate to ground and center your energy. You can place a stone on or near your body if you are healing a specific illness or disease or trying to manifest energy.

Crystals are energy, vibrating at their particular frequency. Like sound, these stones have different vibrations that affect our bodies differently. You align yourself with that stone's vibration by choosing one, or many, to help you with a certain goal. Each stone has a distinct vibration, and if you want to seek a particular effect or heal a specific ailment, you can choose a stone that emits healing vibrations or contains certain healing qualities.

Essential oils

A close cousin to meditation is aromatherapy, also called essential oil therapy, which aims to promote mental and spiritual well-being through essential oils. These oils are useful in helping cure disease, support the immune system, improve mood, encourage relaxation, and create an overall balance in our body. The practice of aromatherapy surrounds the idea of our sense of smell sending messages to our brain that then trigger our emotional responses to the smells. Thus, aromatherapy helps us break old patterns and create mental transformation. You can use aromatherapy by using candles, burning resins, incense sticks, or dropping essential oils onto a diffuser. You can use all of these methods for chakra healing.

You can use essential oils to treat both the subtle energy body and the physical body. They smell pleasant and can help ease muscle tension and treat specific types of pain. Your energetic body consists of meridians and chakra points, each with unique healing qualities. You can balance your physical chakras through associated body chakras and chakras that flow to that physical organ.

Chakra healing through aromatherapy can help us achieve mental and spiritual well-being. It is another way to self-heal and achieve equilibrium. This practice can help balance your emotions and mental states, let go of negative emotions, break old habits, and transform how you think and feel.

Essential oils are used for more than just their pleasant scent. They help us connect with our chakras and create healing on various levels. Applying 5 to 6 drops to a certain chakra can ground, center, release, or open it. You can enhance the healing experience by combining meditative practice after applying the essential oils. As you drift away into your meditation, the vibration of the oil can release blockages in the chakra, allowing the energy to flow more freely. This item can help you balance your chakras and promote overall well-being.

It is a type of subtle energy that surrounds the body, and imbalances of this energy can negatively affect our mental, emotional, and spiritual health.

Essential oils are easily accessible and can be used in many ways to heal the body. You can place a drop of some oils in a small bowl of water and add it to a diffuser to fill your house with the healing power of these fragrances.

Your Sacred Healing Space

People have practiced creating a sacred space or altar, regardless of their culture or belief, since the beginning of existence. This place helps when you need quiet time to reflect on your day. For some people, creating a sacred space can make you feel closer to a deity of your choosing or connect to the earth you see around you. However, using your space in this way can have other positive results, too, as it helps you focus on yourself and allows your mind to stay clear. It can help you unwind and clear your mind of other things weighing you down.

Creating a sacred space can work wonders for our chakra healing. It brings us closer to ourselves and gives us a sense of community and comfort. One tip for creating a sacred space is to ensure the decor reflects who you are as a person or how you define yourself. For example, add seashells and beach-related decor to your room if you are a sea lover. Bring natural elements like tree branches, flowers, plants, and sea rocks if you are a nature lover. Having items like this around your room can bring a sense of calm and peace into your life. Our sacred healing spaces should always be places that inspire creativity and help us feel comfortable and calm, especially at night when we are very relaxed. Keep the space clean and organized to avoid cluttering.

You can place a few crystals by your computer, laptop, or mobile device to create a more balanced workspace. Set up a workplace crystal grid to create a protective field, like black tourmaline or onyx, to absorb negative energy. You can also use geodes or clear quartz for healing and clarity. A row of hematite stones over your laptop can also help keep any dangerous energy away.

Try these crystals next time you are feeling especially scattered or confused.

If you don't wear jewelry, place a few crystals on your nightstand. The healing crystals could be placed on the third eye, throat, and heart chakra to improve communication, focus, and creativity. You can slip a tumbled amethyst stone under your pillow to bring vivid dreams and promote a good night's sleep. Modern witches and spiritually awakened people place selenite shards around their homes to clear negative energy and enhance other crystals' capabilities. You can also place small pieces of amethyst or rose quartz in the corners of the house or any room to create a protective and safe space. Additionally, you can place hematite around doorways to keep negativity from entering.

Daily rituals help us to maintain a spiritual connection every morning or night before bedtime to clear out any funky or stagnant energy in the body. Keeping a ritual sacred space for your home or meditation space allows you to envelop yourself in the positive energy as you engage in your ritual or touch base with your higher self. Adding candles, crystals, and fragrance oils to your altar or sacred space helps you stay grounded in your smaller sacred space as you travel to the bigger playing field of life. Having a special place to call your own helps you keep energy within your personal space and center, centers yourself, and brings your higher self into the present moment.

Chapter 4: Maintaining a Daily Balance in Life

Regularly cultivating mindfulness and practicing gratefulness allows you to stay in the present and show up fully for yourself. Cultivating a daily balance in life involves different aspects of your life. These aspects include your relationships with others, physical health, and spiritual life. It is important to care for these areas of your life equally. For everything else, evolve your practice slowly and see the changes as they happen, using your altar as your guide in your daily balance in life. Keeping yourself balanced naturally is a practice that takes patience and dedication over time.

Sometimes it is easy to put others first, neglect to take care of yourself, or even forget to exercise. If the chakras are out of balance, your body's energies cannot flow freely. Maintaining a daily routine and adding meditation and chakra healing can bring positive movement into your life and help naturally balance each aspect of your health and consciousness. Here are a few other ways to help you maintain a daily balance in life through the world's hustle:

Epsom salt baths are good for highly sensitive people and those with physical aches and pains. They also help clear auras, soothe muscular and other physical pains, and manage stress. You can partner your warm bath with flower petals, scented candles, and essential oils to better set your mood and further your healing process. Salt baths can relieve tension, stress, and pain and calm the mind. These baths can also help you sleep better and ease the discomforts associated with PMS or other hormonal imbalances.

Long walks can help release stress. After a long day, take a walk along the beach or through a nearby forest for a change of scenery. The fresh air is a nice release and helps you clear your mind. You can also listen to soothing music as you stroll along. Walking does wonders for the mind and the body. It sends out a message of continual movement that translates to a different mental capacity on our endless journey through life.

Declutter your space as you notice your house items build up around you. To keep living quarters free of negative or stale energies, keep a clean home and clutter to a minimum. Utilize your time at home to go through clothes and get rid of clothes that don't fit or do not fit your lifestyle. We can all benefit from this practice. In the feng shui tradition, this helps us let go of things we do not want and keeps our minds free of unnecessary baggage. Whatever you choose to do to maintain your space, make sure you feel comfortable and that you allow the energy to flow naturally.

Smudging is a way to cleanse smaller spaces and remove negative energy. Smudging can be done by weaving together dried herbs, herbs, or leaves of fragrant plants in a bundle and lit to smoke out negative energy from your environment. It is used in conjunction with a consecrated area or certain ritual practices or ceremonies. White sage is a herb used by Native Americans for its powerful clearing properties. To smudge a living space or ourselves, light a bunch of sage and waft the smoke around the room, blessing all items along the way. You can also use Palo Santo to smudge the place and bring positive energies into it.

Relationships play a huge role in our well-being and influence our daily balance. Keeping your energy balanced, grounded, and aligned with others and yourself is important. Removing toxic people in your life can bring your energies back into balance and nourish your soul. It is also helpful to take the initiative in relationships that no longer serve you and create healthy boundaries that allow you to release unhealthy energies into your life consciously. Remember that your relationships can nourish you or keep you in a place of neglect and stagnation that you do not want to be in.

Limit your social media interactions to a few minutes each day to stay in touch with friends and family. Although Instagram and Facebook are full of information, it is not all good vibes or true honesty. Use these tools sparingly to keep in touch with the people you care about the most for a quick check-in rather than to post photos or long updates. Don't give inflated appraisals about your favorite book, restaurant, movie, place, event, or experience just so that others have something to like or comment on.

The power of daily practice takes time to build. A daily practice of meditation, new career goals in life, taking care of our bodies through exercise, and healthy food choices all take time to implement. A daily practice of cultivating energy for the chakras, adding flower essences and essential oils to your altar and living space, and increasing your mindfulness through exercise, gratitude, and mindful meditation will reap benefits over time as you grow spiritually and ground yourself in everyday reality.

Connect to nature through walks along the beach, through nature trails, or simply taking a moment in your garden or backyard, which all help us ground ourselves and connect us to our spiritual selves. Nature energy is essential to our well-being. All the plants, animals, and minerals are alive and provide us with natural energy that we can benefit from on our journey through life. Getting in touch with nature is the first step to maintaining your balance in life. Reiki is an energy healing technique that uses universal life force energy to channel the healing energy to the recipient. It can often be used for self-healing and can help ease pain, stress, tension, anxiety, and fear. Reiki is a natural energy that helps balance each chakra. It helps us feel empowered and keeps us centered and balanced daily.

Laugh, smile, and enjoy the little things in life. Don't take yourself too seriously, and have a good time. Take a moment to appreciate the little things in life. Whether changing a light bulb or painting a room, make space for joy and laughter in your life. A daily routine of laughter, humor, and happiness will help bring more joy into your life and keep you grounded and balanced. Laughter has been proven in the medical field to improve your mood and influence others to think positively. Laughter stimulates the immune system, increases your energy level, and even lowers your blood pressure.

Cook a delicious meal or treat yourself to a nice meal at a restaurant you enjoy. Eating well is an essential part of keeping our physical selves healthy. Eating food that makes you feel energized and nourished will lead to added energy and joy in your life. Food is an expression of our physical being and what we put into our bodies affects our energy in our daily lives. Maintaining a daily life balance through regular gentle exercise, easy breathing techniques, and eating well improves well-being and allows for a more peaceful spirit. Nourishing your body with whole foods and nurturing yourself with the right nutrients are great ways to be healthy inside and out. Eating a variety of foods is important as part of staying healthy. Eating whole organic foods is even better. The more you nourish your body with healthy options, the more energy you can channel into other areas of your life. It is all about balance. If you don't take time for yourself, you don't have time for others. Maintaining your daily eating routine helps you reclaim time, stay focused, and be more productive throughout the day. Healthy living is an essential component of your spiritual well-being.

Practice thanking the Universe. Find small ways to express gratitude every day. Write in a journal, share your appreciation with those around you, or make time to meditate and express gratitude for the good things in life. The practice of daily gratitude will help you move through life with a sense of appreciation for the simple things in life. Gratitude is an energy that can move you forward in life and help you maintain your balance.

The Power of Yoga

Yoga *asanas* or poses are physical postures held for set periods that help open the chakras and balance the body's energy flow. Kundalini yoga uses specific physical poses, chanting, breathing techniques, and meditation to awaken the Kundalini energy. Each type of yoga facilitates a different state of consciousness. Yoga practices can help balance body energy while calming the mind. Regularly practicing yoga will help to ground you and center your thoughts. It is a great way to start your day; it helps your body move from a restful state into a more alert and focused state. Yoga and meditation are two of the most well-known methods for achieving wholeness and a balance between body, mind, and spiritual health.

Yoga helps to bring vital life force into the chakras, create awareness and open the chakras. It also helps to ground us in our bodies through a sensory experience and brings attention to how our postures affect how we move through the world. This can be especially helpful to highly sensitive people. Yoga also helps us build focus and strength for our nervous system. These poses can also help you establish mindfulness in your body and the present moment. Restorative yoga is meant to replenish and rejuvenate your body and spirit following hard work or physical activity. This yoga type also helps quiet the mind and offers complete relaxation. Ideal to do before bed or as a nighttime practice, restorative yoga can help you fall asleep more peacefully at night.

Kundalini awakens from the base of the spine and moves up the chakras through the torso into the head. Traditionally, the Kundalini energy moves up through the spine in sets of seven spinal locations called chakras. The chakras in our body affect our health, emotions, and even our thinking. The chakras are connected with the endocrine and nervous systems, which deliver messages to our brains to help us interpret sensory information. When energy, or *prana*, is blocked in the chakras, our health can be negatively affected, leading to different illnesses we experience daily and can lead to more serious long-term disorders. Kundalini yoga practitioners believe that Kundalini energy is spiritual and physical, is influenced by our thoughts and emotions, and is connected to our psyche, our being, and the unconscious. The Kundalini energy moves through the chakras in progressive stages of awakening. Awakening is a process best understood sequentially and awakening our body's energy systems. When Kundalini's energy awakens and our chakras heal, it increases our capacity to think deeply and gain insight into human behavior and motivation.

Chakras are invisible body energy centers that work together to balance your spiritual self. Yoga can balance and open your chakras, which is important for your well-being. Yoga helps open the chakras, which affect your physical well-being and helps you connect more deeply to yourself and the world around you.

Yoga requires a lot of physical movement and can be relaxing. It can also help people practice healthier eating habits and other positive lifestyle changes. Yoga helps us cultivate balance in our lives and teaches us to take responsibility for our bodies and minds while opening us up to the vast universal energy around us.

Try different types of yoga to see what works best for you at that moment. The common thread is balance and connecting the mind and the body. This way is simple but powerful to balance your life and energy. The relationship between your physical body and your moods and relationships is complicated to attend to daily. While yoga helps us ground and connect with our bodies and the earth, we can also practice mindfulness through yoga postures and meditation techniques.

Yoga classes can be expensive and may not fit into everyone's schedules. It also takes time to achieve optimal results and requires self-study and the cultivation of stillness. You can do your research on yoga poses and find videos online to help you get started.

Chapter 5: Illnesses from Imbalanced Chakras

In this chapter, you will use self-healing techniques to address common ailments associated with imbalanced chakras. These techniques will help you restore vital energies to specific chakras by determining the root causes of the imbalances and using the appropriate healing tools.

Common Symptoms and Ailments

When something feels off, you may experience the first signals through emotional, mental, and spiritual symptoms. These symptoms can range from simple issues like neck pain to more complicated issues like addiction. Here are a few illnesses that can manifest through an imbalanced chakra system:

Addiction

Affected chakras: throat chakra, may relate to other chakra blockages

When addicted to a substance, you feel silenced, unable to express yourself, and have lost communication with yourself and others. This addiction is usually due to a lack of energy or an imbalance of one or more chakras. Addictions typically develop as compensations for our deep-rooted feelings that we are not enough. This event usually arises when we are hurt, abused, neglected, or have been taught to bury our emotions, like by stuffing our feelings with food, drugs, or alcohol. Many spiritual paths teach that the best way to stop the addictive cycle is to stop feeling mad at ourselves or that others have done something wrong to us. When other people share the blame with themselves, it helps us realize that we are not the center of the universe or the main reason things go wrong in our lives. Addicts are motivated by their need for love and approval; it is through their addictions that they try to get love from those around them. When your addictions stop bringing joy and fulfillment, you look inward and question your true value in life. Addiction can be related to the following:

- The Heart Chakra: you repress our feelings, so they no longer flow easily and freely through you.

- The Sacral Chakra: you feel ashamed of who you are or self-medicating yourself through painful emotions.

- The Root Chakra: you feel like addiction is the only way to survive, or you do not feel grounded.

Adrenal fatigue

Affected chakras: Root chakra, Sacral Chakra, Solar Plexus Chakra

Adrenal fatigue occurs when our adrenal glands become taxed by the constant heightened stress response, rendering adrenal health insufficient. The adrenal gland controls the internal and external response to stress. Adrenal fatigue can cause the adrenal glands to become overtaxed and exhausted to depletion. This state of exhaustion prevents the body from healing and repairing itself. Addison's disease is a severe form of adrenal failure that can be life-threatening if not treated promptly.

Some signs of adrenal fatigue include general tiredness, body aches, unexplained weight loss, low blood pressure, lightheadedness, loss of body hair, and skin discoloration. Stress can push your adrenal system into overdrive, resulting in exhaustion and fatigue. Excessive stress causes the body to produce more adrenaline and cortisol, the hormones that fuel the stress response. When stress is ongoing, your body becomes accustomed to this state, and your adrenal glands become exhausted from overwork. Adrenal fatigue is common in today's fast-paced world of constant electronic communications and rapid change.

Anger

Affected chakras: Root chakra, may relate to other chakra blockages

When you are angry, the source is often fear. If your safety, livelihood, or survival is threatened, your anger may resonate with the root chakra. It may also affect the crown, third eye, or sacral plexus chakra. Anger can be rooted in several triggers:

- isolation

- feeling unsupported

- being ignored

- being taken advantage of

- feeling overwhelmed

- feeling misunderstood

The root chakra center contains your survival instincts and feelings of security. You might feel threatened when your values are attacked. When your survival instincts are challenged, anger overpowers all other feelings. Anger is your defense mechanism to protect you from external threats. Some are more vulnerable than others to feeling angry when threatened. The imbalance of your chakra can result in anger that surfaces in unexpected ways and will not necessarily resolve easily by changing your point of view. When your feelings become overwhelmed by fear, your root chakra center can become blocked, causing your feelings to manifest in anger.

Anorexia and Bulimia

Affected chakras: Solar Plexus Chakra

Anorexia and bulimia are eating disorders characterized by abnormally low body weight and a distorted perception of one's weight. Bulimia, on the other hand, is a tendency to binge on large amounts of food followed by compensatory behaviors intended to suppress the food, called purging. Both eating disorders are characterized by extreme control of food intake and weight, often to the point of starvation and self-harm. Both of these disorders result in an out-of-balance solar plexus chakra.

Anorexia and bulimia are associated with extreme feelings of self-hatred and may be associated with anxiety disorders and depression.

Anxiety

Affected chakras: All chakras possibly affected

Anxiety is a feeling of intense, excessive, and persistent worry that can permeate our everyday existence and cause panic attacks. Anxiety is an expression of fear associated with a lack of energy in the sacral chakra, meaning that emotional issues become difficult to handle. This chakra is the center of our being and reflects the qualities of love and compassion. When you experience a fear of rejection or abandonment, you do not trust that you are okay no matter what or when others reject you. You often react by overdoing it. Anxiety can make you feel out of control and uncomfortable in your body. It is often associated with stressful situations, such as a new job or relationship, or worrying about future events and situations.

Depending on your anxiety, an imbalance in any of the chakras may be involved, such as the crown chakra if we feel like the

Divine Being or the Universe does not have our back or the third eye if we do not trust our intuition.

Asthma and Allergies

Affected chakras: Heart chakra

When you experience allergies or narrowing airways, it can affect your quality of life and cause respiratory distress and inflammation in your skin, airway, sinuses, or digestive system. Allergies can be caused by overly sensitive immune systems and are commonly caused by overexposure to airborne particles or chemicals. Allergens may include pollen, mold, dust, and other particles that irritate the sinuses and trigger an exaggerated immune response causing inflammation. Everyone has an immune system to fight foreign invaders, such as viruses and bacteria. If too many allergens bombard your body, your immune cells can overreact and attack harmless substances in our environment, such as foods, pollen, and house dust mites. It can also result from a chakra imbalance in the heart chakra, which handles loss, love, compassion, or emotional pain.

Back Pain

Back pain not caused by physical trauma or repetitive physical stress may signify chakra health. The chakra that requires healing can be classified by which region of the back the pain is coming from.

Upper back

Affected chakras: Heart chakra

When feeling unloved, unsupported, or holding back love, we may feel pain in the upper back. People who often repress their feelings of anger suffer from back pain. The imbalance of your throat chakra may have you speaking only when necessary and creating a wall of silence when communicating. Heavy emotions and dysfunctional relationships can cause the aura of your heart chakra to feel blocked and restricted. Some physicians often call this cervical strain.

Middle back

Affected chakras: Heart chakra

When you have issues around love, feeling loved, holding onto past hurts, or anger, an imbalance in your heart chakra may be triggered, and you may experience tension or pain in the middle back.

Lower back

Affected chakras: Sacral chakra, root chakra

When we feel challenged in our relationships, creative expression, or survival, an imbalanced root chakra can become tense in the lower back. An unbalanced sacral chakra can cause tension and pain in the back when emotionally blocked or restricted.

Cancer

Affected chakras: All chakras affected

Cancer occurs when abnormal cells develop and divide uncontrollably, infiltrating and destroying normal body tissue. It can occur on many levels and result from an imbalance in various, if not all, chakras. Cancer symptoms include pain, fatigue, loss of appetite, frequent urination, weight loss, fever, swelling in the lymph nodes, and anemia. Successful cancer treatment depends on the cancer stage and your unique condition. There is a range of therapies and treatment plans for cancer that you may use in combination with methods such as acupuncture and magnetic therapies. Cancer happens when your negative energy has been stagnant, which acts like the disease as it eats away at itself.

Common cancer manifestations in the body:

- Crown chakra: Brain tumors

- Throat chakra: Lung, thyroid, laryngeal cancer

- Heart chakra: Lung, breast, esophageal cancer

- Solar plexus chakra: Pancreatic, stomach, liver, colon cancer

- Sacral chakra: Colon, ovarian, endometrial cancer

- Root chakra: Rectal, prostate cancer

Codependency

Affected chakras: Root chakra, sacral chakra, solar plexus chakra, heart chakra

Codependency is a dysfunctional, one-sided relationship where one partner sacrifices their needs to help the other and is often based on the fear of abandonment and rejection. This relationship has a direct link to the root chakra. You may exhibit codependency behaviors by placing yourself in relationships that are unhealthy or even destructive for you. You may feel controlled by your partner or loved ones when trying to maintain a co-dependent relationship. Your extremely powerful root chakra's attachment to your emotions becomes polarized by an experience of a sense of lack. You also feel abundant energy when your partner's behavior coincides squarely with what you desire.

Codependency affects the heart chakra, the solar plexus chakra, and the sacral plexus chakra. This event can lead to a lack of discernment in relationships. Being dependent on your partner often arises from childhood, when the root chakra is blocked and dysfunctional. The reversal flow of energy in the lower chakras impedes your ability to rely on yourself.

Conflict

Affected chakras: Sacral plexus chakra, solar plexus chakra, throat chakra

When we conflict with someone or something, we try to be heard, express ourselves, and communicate what we feel. The throat, solar plexus, and sacral chakras are involved. This emotional exchange heightens our anxiety, and we can become self-conscious or defensive. When we feel emotionally repressed or depleted, we may tend to suppress our feelings. When these emotions are trapped in our lower chakras and not expressed freely, we may experience relationship disharmony and arguments.

Constipation

Affected chakras: Root chakra, solar plexus chakra

Difficulties in bowel movements may indicate a root chakra dysfunction. It may also be helpful to consider whether you feel triggered by survival issues causing stress. The sacral chakra may affect elimination through the lower back or hips when lower chakras are blocked or overenergized. The emotional elements connected to the solar plexus and sacral plexus chakras come into play when we become resistant to defecation. It can signify an emotional conflict in the solar plexus and sacral chakras, leading you to resist pleasure or avoid defecation.

Depression

Affected chakras: Crown chakra, Solar Plexus, and heart chakra.

Depression can occur for many reasons, including temporary passing through or being a constant presence in our lives. It can also affect our appetite and our sleep. Depression and anxiety, and other emotional disorders indicate poor chakra health. Depression may result from a root chakra imbalance in which the lower chakras are overenergized.

Depression is often confused with sadness, though there are differences. Sadness and grief are natural responses to the loss of any kind and feel passive, whereas depression is active. Depression is not a sign of weakness; it's an illness. Understand that depression is a physical condition that can be managed and controlled. When our thoughts of self-worth are low, we become more susceptible to depression. Recognize the importance of putting your wellness first and the motivation to care for yourself without feeling guilty or weak.

Emotional baggage is a heart chakra issue, where the past is projected onto the present. The sacral chakra may be affected when the sacral lower chakra is blocked or reversed circulation in the lower chakras, leading to feelings of lack and being on an emotional rollercoaster. We may feel empty when feeling unsupported, unloved, or holding back love. These feelings of undervaluing are also felt in the throat and heart chakras.

When we are depressed, we usually feel lonely and disconnected from the rest of the world and even have anger toward the Divine. This emotion is an indication that our crown chakra is out of harmony. A key way to manage depression is to engage in regular physical activity that helps lift your spirits and resolve unresolved feelings. You may also benefit from guided meditations or hypnotherapy. You should avoid seclusion and isolation. Be social and engage in activities that make you feel more upbeat. You can also attend support groups as a platform for sharing your story and gaining encouragement and interaction. The more connected you feel to your world and the people around you, the better you can manage your depression.

Digestive Issues

Affected chakras: Solar plexus chakra

When you feel low self-esteem, intimidation, or powerlessness, the solar plexus chakra becomes imbalanced, resulting in digestive issues. The sacral chakra and solar plexus can interact, leading to feelings of self-pity, frustration, and betrayal. Digestive symptoms may range from abdominal cramping and constipation to diarrhea and nausea. An overactive root chakra also affects digestion; therefore, poor food choices and overeating may be a factor in digestive difficulties.

Disconnect from Self and Others

Affected chakras: Heart chakra, root chakra

When disconnected from who you are, how you feel, and what lights you up, your heart chakra is out of balance; this often displays frustration with not feeling connected with others and general discontent about life. If you feel lonely or become detached from others, you may suppress emotion in your root chakra, resulting in numbness and disconnection from others. If your root chakra is overactive, you may feel disconnected from others until you get something you want. You may feel disconnected inside or from other people in your life. If you feel disconnected from yourself and others, this can make it difficult to deal with emotions. You may become irritated or angry about situations or the things you perceive as wrong or unfair. You may judge people impulsively and react aggressively.

Fatigue

Affected chakras: Solar plexus chakra, crown chakra

Fatigue is related to the solar plexus chakra, our power center. If you are prone to adrenal fatigue, addicted to being busy, or habitually overwork yourself, you are driving yourself into fatigue due to solar plexus chakra imbalance. Overwork and undervaluing yourself can leave you feeling depleted and tired despite getting more accomplished. When overused and underperforming, your body goes into survival mode and shuts down, creating fatigue. When you feel overstressed and overwhelmed, your immune system weakens, leaving you at risk for disease.

Fear

Affected chakras: Root chakra, sacral chakra, solar plexus chakra

When you feel fear, you see it as someone or something dangerous; this causes a change in brain and organ function, activating a cascade within our sympathetic nervous system that brings us into fight-or-flight mode, which can negatively impact our lives. Fear of abandonment can lead to anxiety in the sacral chakra repelling others from your life. We may feel unworthy of being loved causing suppression of emotion and disconnection from ourselves and others. The root chakra can also be affected by fear. It may be caused by Genghis Khan syndrome, where we feel inadequate and powerless to fight or survive. This effect can cause fear and insecurity. The solar plexus chakra can also become blocked or reversed during fear of abandonment, leading to the fear of not having enough resources to feel cared for or be loved.

Financial Issues

Affected chakras: Solar plexus chakra, heart chakra

Financial issues may arise when our self-esteem is lacking. We may have a strong need to buy to feel good about ourselves or to avoid feeling vulnerable. A withdrawal of resources from the root chakra creates fear about survival, which can cause financial instability and worries. The solar plexus chakra is affected by our attachment to money and how we are affected by money. Our confidence is negatively affected when we lack financial stability. We cannot cope with life's challenges when we're worried about paying the bills. Our self-worth is affected when we cannot provide for ourselves and others. This effect can also influence our confidence, causing low self-esteem. The imbalance of the heart chakra may cause rejection of belief in a higher source or Divine intervention in our daily lives. This imbalance can cause us to seek solutions, which may involve spending money. You may feel you should be using money and everything you own to achieve your perception of success.

Grief

Affected chakras: Heart chakra

When we lose someone we love, it is healthy to grieve. However, if the grief is left unprocessed for too long, it can cause a block in the heart chakra, making us feel lonely, lose hope, or cultivate bitterness. Unprocessed grief can cause us to withdraw and become detached from others. If this becomes a pattern, it can affect our root chakra, making disconnection from the Divine the primary goal in life. We can experience grief as a result of the death of a loved one. You may also be grieving from losing a job, health, home, or relationship, significantly affecting your daily life. This type of grief usually stems from unresolved emotions rooted in the heart chakra. Have compassion for yourself during grief. Give yourself time to heal, reconnect with others, and soothe your heart chakra with Light energy and affirmations.

Guilt

Affected chakras: Sacral chakra, solar plexus chakra

Guilt is an emotion related to the sacral plexus chakra, which is the seat of our emotions. Guilt can affect our self-esteem and sense of power, affecting the solar plexus chakra. If we feel guilty about not accomplishing what we were capable of accomplishing, this can cause a lack of self-belief that affects productivity. Suppose we feel guilty about not living up to the expectations of others. In that case, this can make us feel inadequate and inferior, resulting in low self-esteem and a compulsive need to prove ourselves to others.. If you feel guilt for feeling negative emotions because you were always raised to suppress negative emotions, this can lead to repression of any emotional response to situations in life. We may feel guilty for being who we are. We can get stuck in guilt, which locks us up inside our heads and prevents us from differentiating our own perspective from the past.

Headache

Affected chakras: Third eye chakra, crown chakra

When we get headaches that aren't directly caused by physical imbalances, it can indicate disharmony in one of our chakras. Third-eye headaches can occur when we ignore our intuition and do not honor our inner wisdom. When we ignore our intuition, the swirling energy in our heart chakra becomes unbalanced as we feel disconnected from our hearts and each other. Disharmony in the crown chakra could cause headaches and pain in the upper back area between the shoulder blades. Headaches can also be related to issues with our mental or emotional states. If we feel depressed or overly stressed, this can affect the brain's chemical balance.

Heartburn

Affected chakras: Heart chakra, sacral chakra, third eye chakra

Heartburn is caused by an imbalance of the heart chakra that can manifest as anger, frustration, or resentment that blocks us from forgiving ourselves or others. Heartburn may also arise from envy or jealousy when the heart chakra becomes imbalanced, caused by a feeling of lack or deprivation. When the heart chakra is blocked, we may become intolerant of criticism or negativity from others. We may also become cynical, suspicious of others' motives, or feel persecuted or attacked. You may find yourself being overly judgmental and hypocritical. Therefore, the lifestyle choices that result in heartburn are usually rooted in the sacral chakra, which is related to body image, or your third eye chakra, which is related to self-worth. If we need to prove ourselves to others through how we look, we may feel inferior to others and want to prove our worth through material gain. If you lack self-worth, you may compensate by listing achievements or accomplishments to prove your value through status. However, when you lack self-worth, you generate emotional imbalances at the heart chakra that can result in heartburn.

Due to an imbalance in the sacral and solar plexus chakras, you may feel resentment or anger that builds up when you are away from the people you love and unable to share your innermost thoughts and feelings. You may feel grief, sadness, anger, or frustration, which has nowhere to go causing stomach pain and discomfort.

Hemorrhoids

Affected chakras: Root chakra, sacral chakra

Hemorrhoids are swollen veins in the anus and lower rectum that a root chakra imbalance may cause. This chakra is all about survival, so it may be related to a fear of letting go, the anger of the past, or feeling burdened. It could be that you feel shameful to talk about your health issues with others, and that guilt causes your ego to manifest physical symptoms to keep you from feeling exposed and shamed.

We may consider the pain and effort required to let go as an inconvenience rather than a chance to heal. We have much to consider when we let go of something, especially something or someone that we wish to keep in our lives. We also have to face the fear of letting go and go through the grieving process, which may bring up unresolved emotions from the past that need to be released for healing. You could also be carrying around other people's baggage from the past.

Hip Discomfort

Affected chakras: Sacral chakra, solar plexus chakra

When you experience tightness, tension, muscle spasms, or pain in the hips, you often have unexpressed emotions in the sacral plexus chakra causing the pain. The rock-and-roll days may have far outweighed our days relaxing and winding down. A sense of imbalance in the sacral chakra may cause a sense of being stuck up in our past, and that's not healthy for the hips. Your hips may be feeling the tension of past emotional trauma that you store. Often, these unresolved emotions can be found in the solar plexus chakra and manifest as criticism, anger, resentment, bitterness, or a judgmental attitude toward others. Forgiveness may be necessary to heal the inner wounds of the past that are causing pain in the hips.

Infertility

Affected chakras: Root chakra, sacral chakra, solar plexus chakra

Infertility occurs when a woman cannot conceive despite frequent attempts for at least a year. A root chakra imbalance may be due to a fear of fertility issues, which can be linked to fearing death. Women may fear that they will not have a child, which may derive from a trauma in the past, such as rape or the death of a child. Some also think that fertility issues can be caused by a conflict between the female and male chakras. For instance, if a woman's female energy instincts are blocked or repressed from her sacral chakra, she may have difficulty conceiving. Imbalances in the sacral chakra may also cause infertility in women, and the navel is the seat of the sacral chakra. Imbalances in the root chakra can cause many difficulties for women. If her sacral plexus chakra is involved, the root and solar plexus chakras are also involved because infertility can trigger issues around family and self-esteem.

Jaw Pain

Affected chakras: Throat chakra

The temporomandibular joint (TMJ) connects your jawbone to your skull and acts like a sliding hinge to open and close the mouth. TMJ pain may be caused by stress in the jaw or a desire to hold back what we want to say. This tie with communication can relate to intolerance and repression of emotions held in your throat chakra. We may hold back what we say because we do not want to hurt someone's feelings or are afraid of rejection or disapproval. Even if we say what we want, we may not say it with kindness because we are too attached to our opinions and prepared to defend them at all costs, which can include biting people down on our opinions. Other causes of jaw pain include clenching, grinding teeth, or holding tension in the jaw.

Leg Pain

Affected chakras: Solar plexus chakra, root chakra

Leg pain is often linked to a root chakra imbalance but can also be linked to the solar plexus chakra. A root-located imbalance of the sacral chakra can cause a fear of death and of moving forward in life, which can create unexpressed fears in other body parts. These fears may be expressed as physical symptoms and can manifest as leg pain. A solar plexus-related imbalance of the sacral chakra may cause an inability to follow through on your decisions and dreams, which could manifest as leg pain.

Loneliness

Affected chakras: Heart chakra, may affect other chakras

The heart chakra wants us to connect with ourselves and with others. But when we have balance in this chakra, we express healthy self-love and self-worth. Why would we isolate ourselves from love? Quite simply, the energies of the other chakras may be unexpressed or blocked from our heart chakra and may need to be healed first. For example, for root chakra issues, we may receive communication from our heart chakra that healing is needed in the sacral plexus chakra. The daughter may have root chakra issues in the relationship with her mother because of her mother's protective behavior. The mom may manifest a sacral chakra imbalance because she has received insufficient love from her daughter.

Neck Pain

Affected chakras: Throat chakra

Neck pain can be caused by an imbalance in the throat chakra caused by holding ourselves back from expressing ourselves freely and openly. We often hold ourselves in that physical and mental grip for fear of being criticized, rejected, or ridiculed for holding a particular point of view. The need to control others and situations is very common among those who strongly believe in their point of view, whether it is based on religion, politics, or spirituality. When a point of view or belief is strongly held for the fear of its disappearance or loss, the throat chakra gets tight, which may result in a headache or neck pain.

Neuropathy

Affected chakras: Third eye chakra

Neuropathy is caused by damage to the nerves, and can result from a traumatic injury, infection, diabetes, side effects of chemotherapy, inherited causes, or exposure to toxins. However, it can also result from an imbalanced third eye chakra. The third eye chakra often becomes imbalanced when we deny our intuition. We may ignore our intuition by thinking that it is a way of craziness or making up stories in our minds. Intuition has a frequency that interferes with the thought process. Therefore, we avoid listening to it because our ego does not want to know. But when we are in doubt, our intuition points us in the right direction. Some things are incurable, but we can manage the damage by supporting our nerves with a healthy diet and lifestyle, meditating, and healing our chakras.

Panic Attacks

Affected chakras: Root chakra, solar plexus chakra, heart chakra

When disconnected from our heart chakra, we can experience panic attacks. These attacks can feel like a punch in the gut because our power center is affected. We feel scared and vulnerable when our heart chakra is out of balance by thoughts such as "I have no power" or "I am not worthy."

Others may feel anger toward you for causing the attacks. If you do not feel in control of the situation, your root chakra may be unbalanced. With an unbalanced root chakra, you may feel trapped and unable to move on. You may have difficulty making decisions and find yourself living an unconscious, difficult life. A lack of inner balance causes the inner alarm system to be triggered more often and leads to a feeling of powerlessness.

These panic attacks can happen when there is a disconnection from your heart chakra. Your root chakra can also be imbalanced when insecure feelings and anger are let off in the wrong direction. The solar plexus chakra is often affected because you live from fear rather than heart-based love by ignoring your inner intuitive guidance system.

Paralysis

Affected chakras: Root chakra, sacral chakra

An altered electromagnetic field can cause paralysis on one side of the body along the spine. This effect can be caused by disease or trauma, such as a car accident. The root chakra and the sacral chakra may be affected if there is a fear of losing control and withering away in the world. If one side of our body is paralyzed, this tells us that our physical self is seen as having little worth.

Schizophrenia

Affected chakras: Throat chakra, heart chakra

Schizophrenia can reflect an imbalanced root chakra related to issues around survival and being. The anxiety caused by an unbalanced throat chakra can also cause mental confusion. An imbalanced heart chakra can create stress, resulting in restlessness that often makes life difficult for those who live with schizophrenia.

Sciatica

Affected chakras: Root chakra, sacral chakra

Sciatica is a painful condition that radiates from the lower back, through the hips and buttocks, and down each leg. The sacral chakra is affected if this severe pain gets out of control and becomes chronic. The sacral chakra may also be affected if it experiences fear regularly.

You can only treat sciatica by treating the cause and using painkilling agents to help reduce the pain level before it worsens. Managing sciatica depends on the seriousness of the cause. Drugs are the first line of treatment, but surgery may be recommended if the hip or back joints are painful and moving has become impossible.

Self-Hate

Affected chakras: Root chakra, solar plexus chakra, heart chakra

Self-hate is based on the perception that we are unlovable and is a result of disconnection from our heart chakra. However, a more frightening idea is that the rest of the world also sees us as unlovable. We feel unworthy of love and shut others out while we are busy manipulating situations to create the necessary conditions for love. When our ego takes center stage, it controls these feelings of unworthiness.

The root chakra is affected when feeling fear of survival. The solar plexus chakra becomes imbalanced because it feels like a bottomless pit of despair due to an overabundance of the need to control others and situations. A healthy heart chakra balances your need to control others and yourself with minimum or no fear. In addition, self-hate is angry energy and emotion, and anger always stems from fear.

Self-Injury

Affected chakras: Root chakra, sacral chakra

Trying to force emotions such as peace and love is sometimes an attempt to heal the pain associated with an unbalanced root chakra. Creating physical pain manifests these emotions outside but can also cause inner pain. Self-injury is a type of self-abuse that is not healthy and may mask underlying issues. The root and sacral chakras are out of balance when this pain gets out of control and becomes chronic. Focusing on thoughts about death can also create an imbalance in the sacral chakra.

Separation Anxiety

Affected chakras: Root chakra, heart chakra

Separation anxiety can be triggered by an unbalanced heart chakra that fears you will lose another opportunity to love. The jealousy associated with a heart out of balance may lead to possessiveness with partners. The sacral chakra often becomes imbalanced as these unbalanced jealous feelings can create intense emotional stress.

This fear felt during separation anxiety discourages us from trying to reach out to others. But the fear of alienating people if we try to connect can limit our social activities. This fear is so strong that it also makes us fearful of dying alone. However, isolation can eventually silence our communication and mutually loving relationships, which is unhealthy. The desire to be with others is important for staying healthy and dying peacefully. Sometimes, separation anxiety is caused by lack of feelings toward others. These unresolved feelings can cause a sense of emptiness that needs to be filled.

Sexual Abuse

Affected chakras: Root chakra, sacral chakra, solar plexus chakra, heart chakra, throat chakra

When we are sexually violated, the abuse can be very damaging, not only to our physical body but to our soul. The root chakra can feel lived on when we have been violated in this way. The sacral chakra may also feel lived in as a result; this is because the throat chakra experiences emotional and spiritual pain that finds its way into physical problems. The solar plexus chakra is also imbalanced as feelings of rejection creep in now that the power center has been violated. A heart chakra out of balance can lead to feelings of guilt and low self-esteem. A strong throat chakra imbalance can limit the expression of feelings. This effect can make it harder for you to seek support from others and makes it likely that you will go unnoticed and unrecognized by those who lack empathy..

Sexually Transmitted Infections

Affected chakras: Sacral chakra, solar plexus chakra

The sacral chakra may be imbalanced if recurring sexually transmitted infections and diseases occur. Unlike the root and solar plexus chakras, which are related to physical survival, the sacral chakra governs our ability to exist and survive.

Sacral chakra deals with our perceptions of sexuality, particularly how we express it and its emotional and physical aspects. When infections occur, your sexual well-being may feel affected. Some infections can be directly related to your sexuality. Repeated infections can indicate imbalances in your emotional expression. When we feel shame, our sacral chakra, which is also where we house feelings about sex and sexuality, is destabilized, and our solar plexus chakra, where we feel our self-esteem, takes a hit.

Sinus Pain

Affected chakras: Third eye chakra

If you are experiencing pain in your sinuses unrelated to allergies, environmental irritants, or direct trauma, you may have an imbalance in your third eye chakra. This chakra helps us trust our intuition beyond physical evidence.

Sinusitis is a painful condition involving swelling and inflammation of the paranasal sinuses. This effect can block the nasal passages, resulting in difficulty breathing. People with problems with their noses are afraid to treat these symptoms due to their embarrassment and the lack of willingness to admit this to others. As a result, exchanging information between heaven and earth gets blocked, and the lungs do not get their proper blood supply. Therefore, the lung energy gets blocked, and the air and energy do not circulate properly.

Skin Issues

Affected chakras: Crown chakra

Skin issues can surface due to an imbalanced crown chakra, resulting in acne, eczema, psoriasis, rosacea, rashes, and dermatitis. All of these conditions are associated with the fourth element of ether. An imbalance in the ether can contribute to the aging process and affect multiple organs in the body. If the crown chakra is out of balance, the ether element cannot deliver good energy to our skin resulting in skin problems.

Sleep Apnea

Affected chakras: Throat chakra

Sleep apnea disrupts the normal breathing pattern during sleep caused by obesity, smoking, sleep apnea syndrome, and thyroid disorders. Sleep apnea may cause fatigue, depression, and memory loss. Sleep apnea may also be caused by emotional stress. An unbalanced throat chakra may prevent the person from expressing feelings, which may result in the physical symptom of sleep apnea. If you or someone you know is suffering from sleep apnea, seek medical help with a practitioner experienced in this work.

Smothering

Affected chakras: Solar plexus chakra, throat chakra

When we fear failure or are obsessed with controlling others to the point where we feel we cannot breathe properly, our solar plexus and throat chakra become imbalanced. Our throat chakra controls communication, yet when we hold our tongue out of fear of being hurt, our throat chakra becomes blocked. This belief can paralyze the ability to speak up and talk out.

If the throat chakra is closed and locked up due to these repressed feelings, it may remain open and receptive to guidance from the spiritual world, but a voice will remain silenced. This event can lead to a lack of support in outer life. In that case, it can lead us to seek unhealthy relationships that offer emotional abandonment as a coping mechanism because we do not feel we have the right to have our needs met or that people truly value what we say.

Stomach Pain

Affected chakras: Solar plexus chakra

Stomach pain and disorders can come in many forms, including ulcers, constipation, diarrhea, inflammatory bowel syndrome or IBS, intestinal problems, indigestion, acid reflux, and gastritis. The stomach illness can also result from feeling overwhelmed, out of control, powerless, intimidated, or lacking self-respect.

Physical pain can impact the solar plexus chakra. If the solar plexus chakra is unbalanced or experiences stress, the organs in the abdomen will be affected by our mental, spiritual, and physical imbalances. Our stomachs may feel tense and become in balance when the solar plexus chakra fully opens up and begins to receive a flow of vital life force.

Stress

Affected chakras: Root chakra, may affect other chakras

Stress is a state of mental tension and emotional strain resulting from very demanding circumstances and problems in our lives, work situations, and relationships. Stress is a nearly unavoidable aspect of modern life. Too much stress can lead to exhaustion of physical resources and cause us to feel dizzy,lightheaded or shaky, irritable, and unable to think or concentrate. Our immune system may start to decline, and we may experience muscle aches. Low immunity to infectious diseases, migraines, and hypertension may also result from ongoing excessive stress. Over time our physical, mental, emotional, and spiritual health can be affected by stress.

Thyroid Disorders

Affected chakras: Throat chakra

The throat chakra is about speaking our truth. Suppose we have disorders in the neck, such as imbalances in the thyroid our throat chakra may be out of balance. Having thyroid imbalances can stop us from uttering our truth. If our voice is muted because of our thyroid imbalances, we may fail to recognize when something is wrong and communicate our symptoms or concerns effectively. This event can lead to inflammation of the throat and result in cough, poor voice quality, sore throat, and even vocal cord paralysis.

Uterine Cysts

Affected chakras: Sacral chakra

Uterine fibroids are non-cancerous growths of the uterus that can cause pain during menstruation, when you have a bowel movement, or when your body is trying to digest food. These cysts are often a signal that the sacral plexus chakra is out of balance. The sacral chakra is the source of sensuality and sexuality. When our sexual energy is blocked, we can develop fibroids or other blockages in reproductive organs.

Weight Issues

Affected chakras: Root chakra, sacral chakra, solar plexus chakra

Although behavioral, lifestyle, exercise, and dietary changes are often addressed for weight issues; another possible cause is a lack of feeling grounded. You may feel unsupported and insecure if your root or sacral chakras are not open. As a result, you may be drawn to food to feel secure.

Your root chakra relates to your sense of stability and grounding; in other words, the ability to be in the flow of abundance and maintain balance no matter what is happening around you. If your root chakra is out of balance, you may feel alone, scared, or depressed, or you may just feel like you are adrift.

When your root chakra is unbalanced, you may feel frustrated, isolated, or fearful. You may become overwhelmed by the demands of life and give in to hopelessness. A balanced root chakra helps us feel connected to nature and secure, and a balanced solar plexus chakra helps us feel powerful.

Chapter 6: Healing Your Root Chakra

The root chakra is about being grounded, secure, and connected to your family and tribe. It is your connection with Mother Earth, so feeling a sense of joy and happiness being physically connected to her and part of a healthy, supportive community is essential to this energetic center. You will be less scattered as your root chakra gets balanced and stabilized. You will find it easier to find grounding within yourself and your space. You will experience more peace and contentment in your life. Protecting yourself, your loved ones, and your tribe will be second nature.

It is essential to your overall health to feel grounded and secure in your existence. A strong feeling of balance at this chakra stabilizes you physically and emotionally, allowing you to feel more centered and anchored in life. It is much easier to get along with people, not become too stressed or overwhelmed, and be at peace within yourself.

If your root chakra is out of balance, you will certainly feel unsettled and uneasy in life. You may have trouble feeling grounded or stable. You may feel insecure or mistrustful of others and life. You may be feeling disconnected from your family or friends. You may also experience anxiety and depression.

Root Chakra Meditation

Here is an easy method of meditation to connect with your root chakra:

1. Sit comfortably with your eyes closed.

2. Breathe deeply and feel your feet firmly rooted into the ground below you, then breathe out and feel your weight dissipate away from the ground and float upward toward the sky with your breath.

3. Bring your attention back to your legs and feet on the floor. Feel them touching the ground and the earth below you. Feel your feet on the ground as you draw your balance from your heels up to your shin bones. Feel your balance in the arches of your feet as gravity pulls you toward the floor.

4. Coordinate the upward pull of your legs with the downward pull of gravity as you meditate on your root chakra. Imagine the breath energizing your perineum. Release anything you may be holding in that area, and ask your root chakra what it needs right now.

5. Allow the downward pull of gravity to anchor you to the Earth. Allow the upward pull of your breath to lift and balance you on the Earth. Feel yourself being held by the Earth with your breath. Feel yourself grounded.

Note: Be patient with yourself, as this practice takes time to get used to. Take breaks whenever you feel any pain in your legs or lower back.

Once you have practiced this meditation for ten minutes, you will feel a sense of calm, peace, and joy rising from your root chakra. You will feel more refreshed and energized. You will feel more grounded and secure. You will no longer feel scattered and anxious as life's events surround you. You will even start to see yourself as a whole, being connected and grounded to the Earth as you elevate your level of consciousness.

Crystals and Stones for the Root Chakra

A great way of bringing feelings of security into your life is by including crystals and gemstones in your healing practices. These stones are powerful allies that vibrate at the same frequency as your root chakra, allowing you to feel connected to Earth while uplifting your spirit and elevating your mind with healing light. Here are some of the crystals and gemstones for balancing the root chakra:

Black Onyx: Onyx is a very powerful crystal for grounding you into reality and connecting you to the Earth. It has strong metaphysical properties that can assist you in finding wisdom and seeing the lessons in situations, as well as locating the truth in any situation. It is like your own psychic antenna that can tap into the frequencies of right and wrong while balancing your root chakra and helping you to be grounded within the Earth.

Rhodonite: This nurturing crystal will help nourish yourself as you nurture your soul through meditation. It will help you feel the comfort you need to settle within yourself and know you are safe and protected within your body and spirit.

Hematite: This stone will help you stabilize your emotions. It will help you feel grounded and secure while uplifting you with a sense of joy and happiness. It will help calm your spirit while stabilizing your thoughts.

Larimar: This stone encourages emotional wholeness and connection to others. Helping you feel connected with your inner self helps you feel connected to others. It promotes kindness and gentleness. It allows you to see life as a lesson and nurtures you as you learn.

Pyrite: Though this stone has a strong feminine energy that provides strength and courage, it is also a stone of great grounding for the Earth. It balances your root chakra and helps you feel that sense of security in your physical body and spirit while feeling safe and protected. It helps encourage your sense of courage and strength in times of trouble.

Smoky quartz: This grounding stone is a brownish grey, translucent variety of quartz crystals, which helps calm your mind, body, and spirit as you focus on grounding yourself through your root chakra. Smokey quartz has strong metaphysical properties and can help you connect with your spiritual guide and intuitive self as you connect with the Earth to ground your being.

Black Tourmaline: Black tourmaline is a beautiful black crystal with protective metaphysical properties that will allow you to sense any negative energy around you. It also cleanses your environment and brings pure energy into your life, allowing you to remain grounded within the Earth even as you work with others or find your tribe.

Selenite: This white crystal brings purity and healing energy into your life as you focus on bringing stability with your root chakra. It purifies your energy field and lifts your energy with positive vibrations and vitality.

Garnet: This reddish-brown stone will balance your root chakra while encouraging strength and courage. It will encourage you to stand up for yourself while feeling connected to those around you.

Lapis Lazuli: Lapis lazuli will help you experience a deep sense of security and peace within yourself. It may stimulate your intellect and creativity while balancing your emotions.

Obsidian: This black or black-and-green stone will make you feel connected to your inner self and security by grounding your root chakra while meditating. It is believed that obsidian can attract helpful spirits to you, which can be very comforting when you need support to get through stressful times. If you meditate, it will help you connect with them easily.

In order to use crystals to connect with your root chakra, clean them first, then charge them with a purification technique or cleanse them with running water. Place the cleaned crystals in a pouch, or place them somewhere you can feel connected to them throughout the day while meditating on your root chakra. You can also place your root chakra crystal on top of your pubic bone and take three slow and deep breaths. You may feel the energy of the crystal pulse or travel to your feet.

Yoga Poses for the Root Chakra

Connect your root chakra to the Earth through yoga poses. These poses will help you easily feel connected and grounded with the Earth while you feel connected within yourself. As you settle into the poses, your body will relax physically while your root chakra relaxes and opens up. They are perfect before bed, or you can do them throughout the day to help you through stressful situations. Each pose is demonstrated below with pictures for your reference:

- **Snake Pose:** Kneel with your hands on the floor. Lift your toes off the floor and your knees off the floor. Reach your hands back toward the floor. On an exhale, lower your chest and forehead toward the floor, lengthening your spine and staying in the pose for 30 seconds. Then, exhale as you push through your heels to return to a kneeling position. Repeat this pose, holding for a total of 1 minute.

- **Calf Stretch:** Come into a standing position. Inhale while lifting your arms above your head. On an exhale, bow forward and draw your left leg back, bending it at the knee and lifting your foot off the floor. Breathe as you bring your right leg forward between the two legs, and then kick out the left foot again so that you are suspended on your toes. Breathe and hold this stretch for 30 seconds. Then, bow forward and inhale as you lower your body back down to the floor, letting go of the pose on an exhale as you lower your body to the floor and step your left leg back into an upright position. Repeat this pose with your right leg, keeping your core muscles engaged as you stay suspended on the toes on your left leg. Repeat this pose for 1 minute 30 seconds, and then repeat this stretch with your right leg.

- **Downward Dog Pose:** Come kneeling with your hands on the floor in front of you at a 90-degree angle. Point your fingers forward. On an exhale, lift your hips and retract them toward the floor as you curl your toes under. Push through your toes and hands as you lift your body to stand, making sure your heels align with your sit bones. On an exhale, bend your knees and push your hips back toward the floor, lowering your body with your fingertips flat on the floor. Then, inhale while pressing your legs and feet back to start again from the kneeling, fingertips forward position. Repeat this pose five times at first, building up over time. You can also do this pose by placing your knees on the floor with your hands flat behind your head as you extend your hips upward.

- **Chair Pose:** Come to a standing position. Place your left foot inside your right yoga block and place your left hand on your block. Bend your right leg, reaching for your right foot with your left hand to maintain balance. On an exhale, reach up toward the sky with your left arm and left arm overhead while reaching back with your right arm down toward the earth. Hold the pose for 30 seconds and switch your stance so your hands reach the opposite way. Repeat for a minute, then release your hands and feet to the floor. Stand in the pose for 3 minutes to feel the sensations throughout your body opening up.

The root chakra is about stability and support. Standing poses, seated postures, and restorative poses can help us surrender to the gravity and groundedness of this chakra.

Essential Oils

Start with these essential oils that will assist your root chakra in opening up and feeling re-energized, grounded, and at peace. These essential oils vibrate at a very earthy frequency that also balances your emotions. They will stimulate your heart and root chakra while cleansing your energy of all negative emotions. These essential oils also promote stability and strength within your body to experience a deep sense of peace and protection.

1. **Vetiver:** Vetiver essential oil is extremely beneficial in grounding you emotionally. It promotes a sense of security and the ability for mental clarity to build your spiritual and emotional foundations. Vetiver essential oil will also clear your chakras of negative energy and promote overall well-being.

2. **Cedarwood:** This essential oil is excellent for grounding and balancing negative emotions. It can also stimulate the root chakra so you can manifest more of what you need while living your life.

3. **Sandalwood:** This essential oil will open your heart chakra and help you let your emotions flow while feeling secure within yourself, and you can feel more connected to those around you. Sandalwood will also clear the energy within your chakras, filling them with the energy of trust and courage.

4. **Frankincense:** This essential oil encourages emotional and spiritual healing and protection. You will also experience emotional stability and openness of the self when connecting with this oil.

5. **Patchouli:** This essential oil promotes emotional balance and allows your spiritual connection to open up within the body.

To connect with the grounding energies of these essential oils, light a white candle and burn your essential oils for 30 seconds to 1 minute. Breathe in the scents as they are burning and allow them to surround you like earthy, calming, uplifting energy. You can also diffuse essential oils for the root chakra if a candle or diffuser is not convenient.

To activate the root chakra, add 5 or 6 drops of essential oil to a dime-size portion of carrier oil, rub your hands together, and place your open palm over your pubic bone. Say something to help you feel grounded and secure in your being and existence. Anoint a crystal with the essential oils or diffuse the oils in your aromatherapy diffuser to experience their healing properties.

Holistic Practices that Balance the Root Chakra

In addition to balancing the root chakra through meditation, yoga, and crystal healing, you can balance it with holistic practices and meditations that use sound to bring you closer to connection within the Earth. These may include:

- **Shamanic Journeying:** Shamanic journeying allows you to journey within yourself. It allows you to contact your spirit guides through meditation.

- **Grounding:** Walking barefoot on the earth, sitting in silence and solitude outdoors many times throughout the day, connecting with nature through gardening or hiking, dancing in a forest, or wandering in the grass.

- **Breathing:** Breathing deeply and fully while feeling the earth's grounding energy through your feet, hands, or crown chakra helps rebalance your root chakra.

- **Massage:** Using massage oil or a sensual oil during your massage can help you feel connected to your root chakra. Having your partner move the oil in circular motions around your hands and feet can help you feel grounded and connected to your body and the Earth.

- **Cooking:** Cooking from raw ingredients allows you the direct connection of not only cooking within Mother Earth but connecting with the foods you eat.

- **Music:** Music that vibrates at a grounding frequency will help you connect to the earth. Music that vibrates at the frequencies of your root chakra will balance the root chakra and bring balance to your body's systems. Music that vibrates at a root chakra frequency is made with deep base notes, such as drum beats, drum circle music, Tibetan Tantric Music, Crystal Temple music, Shamanic drumming, and chanting the sound "LAM". Discovering ways to help you feel more at home within yourself will help you settle into your roots.

Chapter 7: Healing your Sacral Chakra

The sacral plexus chakra is about connecting with your emotions, creative expression, and sexuality. Physically, this chakra is associated with the kidneys, bladder, adrenal glands, and genital organs.

This chakra also focuses on abundance in healthy ways. The methods of meditation, crystal healing, yoga poses, and essential oils will help your sacral chakra to be balanced and open. The connection of this chakra is personal and private. It's deeply connected to feeling in control of your life and what you create. This chakra holds the energy for the reproductive system and the life it can create. When this chakra is imbalanced, you may feel shame for these parts of yourself.

The focus of allowing yourself to feel deeply and openly when dealing with your issues will heal you and allow you the freedom to create in your way. Achieving balance in the sacral chakra is about learning how to create abundance and creatively express your sensual energy.

Sacral Chakra Meditation

The sacral chakra helps align your conscious thoughts with your emotions. When unbalanced, you may feel disconnected from your feelings and make decisions based on logic rather than emotion.

Here is an easy visualization and meditation method to connect with your sacral chakra:

- Find a quiet space where you won't be disturbed.

- Take a few deep breaths to relax your body.

- Slowly inhale through your nose while focusing on the sacral chakra.

- Hold your breath for a few seconds and visualize a bright yellow light from the navel area.

- Imagine a bright golden sun sitting at the center of your abdomen. Feel the colors of orange and yellow radiating from this brightly shining star. The rays of this shining star are absorbed into your navel and spread to the lower abdomen and then to your hips and the pelvis. Feel the orange and yellow light growing bigger and bigger as it moves down to your reproductive organs and then the inner thighs.

- As you inhale, imagine this warm yellow light around your reproductive organs, thighs, and buttocks, relaxing the muscles with intense love, nurturing, and healing energy. As you exhale, try to feel this warm glow spreading to the rest of your body and then visualize it expanding into your surroundings.

- Inhale again slowly while visualizing this light growing bigger and expanding to the skin of your pelvic area and then to your reproductive organs. This glowing yellow light will heal your pain and sadness that block you from abundance. Feel that the light is expanding to the external world on a subconscious level. Imagine a feeling of freedom and joy subconsciously flowing into the world as you continue breathing normally and deeply.

Note: Practicing meditation requires patience, as it takes time to get used to it. Take breaks when you feel any strain in your lower back.

Crystals and Stones for the Sacral Chakra

Crystals that resonate with the sacral plexus chakra include carnelian, amber, moonstone, calcite, orange tourmaline, and sunstone. To work with crystals, cleanse them by smudging them with white sage or palo santo, laying them out overnight under the moonlight, or soaking them in salt water. Here are a few crystals that can help balance your sacral chakra:

Carnelian: It is powerful for releasing fear, anxiety, and negative brainwave patterns. Carnelian helps you amplify your internal feeling of self-worth and self-love.

Amber: This powerful healing stone calms your nerves and emotions. It balances your hormones and stimulates circulation and a release of negative energies. The rays of amber can also help alleviate anxiety and depression, healing any other negative emotions.

Moonstone: The moonstone is a powerful stone for balancing your masculine and feminine energies. It improves the digestive process, clears the chakras, and balances your emotions.

Orange Calcite: This translucent stone enhances your energy and vitality. It harmonizes your body and spirit by stimulating personal power and confidence. Orange calcite creates a feeling of optimism for a more creative, balanced, and abundant lifestyle.

Ruby Stone: Ruby stone is perfect for opening the sacral chakra, helping open you up to feelings of creativity and sexual energy. Ruby stone can help you manifest wealth and abundance through creativity.

Citrine: Citrine is the stone of confidence, creativity, self-esteem, self-love, and personal power. It promotes abundance, productivity, and success in all your life areas.

Sunstone: This bright stone awakens your creative life force and replenishes your power and energy. Sunstone induces a feeling of free self-expression and helps you open up to abundance in all areas of your life. It stimulates the sacral chakra to bring about new ideas, creativity, and confidence.

Tigers Eye: Tigers Eye helps boost self-esteem and energy. It can easily retrieve the confidence and strength you need to pursue your creative dreams with ease.

Goldstone: Goldstone has golden energy, which helps with abundance and prosperity. Goldstone stimulates the sacral chakra and helps release its blockages.

Get into a comfortable seated or lying down position. Hold the crystal in your left hand - the receiving hand - and allow your mind and heart to open to receive any feedback that may flow through. Close your eyes and start with the following affirmation: "I allow my sacral chakra to open up." While repeating this affirmation, place the crystal on your sacral chakra. You can place the crystal anywhere on your abdomen that is comfortable for you. While lying down, you can place your sacral chakra crystal two inches below your navel. Take three slow, deep breaths, and enjoy the crystal's energy.

Yoga Poses for the Sacral Chakra

Practicing yoga helps to heal the sacral chakra and opens it up to love, creativity, and abundance. Here are some yoga postures that will help balance the sacral chakra:

- **Reclined Bound Angle Pose:** This pose stretches the thighs and pelvis and enhances the energy flow in the sacral region. To perform this pose, lie down. Place your palms on your tummy hip-width apart. Lift and bend your knees and slowly let your legs fall to one side. Position your legs in such a way that they come right next to one another. Hold the pose for up to five minutes, and then relax. Practice this pose daily.

- **Yoga Squat:** The yoga squat does wonders for the sacral chakra as it helps in opening the hips and increasing blood flow to the lower abdomen. It helps balance the hormonal secretions and improves digestion. To do this pose, stand with your feet hip-width apart. Bend your knees and sit back as if you were about to sit in a chair. As you squat, ensure your knees are wide apart and not pointed inwards. Focus your attention on your navel. Inhale deeply and straighten your legs. Hold your breath and lower your thighs as far as you can comfortably reach down. Bend your knees as you exhale and return to the original position. Repeat the pose three to five times.

- **Cobra Pose:** The cobra pose increases blood circulation in the lower abdomen, which relieves constipation and depression. It helps increase energy, stamina, sexual vitality, and strength. This pose also increases flexibility. To perform this pose, lie face down and place your hands under your shoulder blades. Slowly raise your upper body while raising your chin and head upward. Hold the pose for a minute, then slowly move your head and body back to the original position.

- **Camel Pose:** This pose increases blood circulation and opens the thighs and the lower back. Stand on your knees at the front of the mat to perform the camel pose. Ensure your knees are hip-width apart in a kneeling position with the tops of your feet on the mat. Then, place your fingertips at the spine's base. As you inhale, lift your gaze and bend backward, expanding up and opening through your sternum. Reach for your heels as you exhale, and let your glutes push forward. Continue taking deep breaths as you hold the pose, then exit the pose by bringing your hands back to your sacrum and slowly rising from your back bend.

- **Lizard Pose:** This pose strengthens the thigh muscles and the abdominal muscles. Lie down with your feet together to do the lizard pose. Spread your toes apart as you lift and straighten your legs. Bend your left knee while stretching your other leg upwards toward the ceiling. Hold the pose for two minutes, then move back to the original position.

- **Cat-cow pose:** The cat-cow pose is a great way to open the sacral chakra. This pose helps stimulate the flow of energy in your sacral chakra and aligns it with your conscious desires. To do this, begin on your hands and knees in a table pose with a neutral spine. As you inhale and move into cow pose, lift your sit bones upward, press your chest forward, and allow your belly to sink. Lift your head, relax your shoulders away from your ears, and gaze straight ahead. As you exhale, come into a cat pose while rounding your spine outward, tucking in your tailbone, and drawing your pubic bone forward. Release your head toward the floor — just do not force your chin to your chest.

Essential Oils

Here are some essential oils that can help open and balance your sacral plexus chakra:

- **Bergamot:** This euphoric oil can help you overcome shyness, increase energy, promote sexual desire, build self-confidence, and increase wealth.

- **Lavender:** This oil helps you overcome sadness and negativity, boost your creativity and confidence, and relieve you from pain.

- **Sandalwood:** This oil helps with emotional healing and stimulates the release of anger and excess energy.

- **Ylang-Ylang:** Ylang-ylang oil has unique properties that help you balance yin-yang energy and increase mental and physical health. It also helps elevate the mood and relieves anxiety, fear, resentment, and tension.

- **Geranium:** Geranium oil helps you feel grounded and relaxed while restoring your energy and self-confidence.

- **Jasmine:** Jasmine oil promotes tranquility and balances emotions. It induces feelings of self-love and calms your mind.

- **Clary Sage:** This oil assists you in overcoming low self-esteem and builds your confidence. It also promotes confidence and inspires you to achieve your dreams.

- **Neroli:** This oil promotes self-confidence, increases love and affection, and helps you get through stress and depression.

- **Cedarwood:** This oil helps you gain self-confidence and helps you overcome emotional stress and tension.

You can anoint your sacral chakra or rub activated oils between your palms to create a connection with it. Say something like, "I now intend to create a connection with my sacral chakra." Then place the oil on your sacral chakra and imagine it spreading through your body.

Holistic Practices that Balance the Sacral Chakra

The sacral plexus chakra is associated with your sense of self-worth. When the sacral chakra is healthy and functioning optimally, you can use its energy to improve your relationships, creativity, emotional balance, abundance, and physical vitality. It can also help you manifest ideas into reality.

The sacral chakra is about sweetness and creativity and can be nurtured through flowing movement and breath. Here are a few other practices that you can do to open your sacral chakra:

- **Tumbling:** Tumbling is a fun activity for your sacral chakra. It not only opens the sacral plexus chakra but also strengthens and balances other chakras.

- **Water therapy:** Going for a swim in the ocean or pool reinvigorates your energy flow to all your chakras.

- **Dancing:** Practice belly dancing, Latin dances such as salsa, and other dances that move the hip area. Such movements can open your sacral chakra and help you connect with your emotions.

- **Tantra:** Learn tantra to get in touch with your sexuality more consciously.

- **Music:** Listening to soothing music or playing music can help you calm your mind and spirit while enticing your sacral chakra to turn its energy toward universal love rather than fear. Chanting the sound "VAM" also helps balance the sacral chakra.

- **Emotional Freedom Technique:** EFT can also be a great way to balance the sacral chakra. It uses finger tapping on certain meridian points to relieve stress and negative emotions from your body and mind.

- **Abdominal massage:** You can massage the sacral plexus chakra area by pressing your hand over your abdomen gently and deeply.

- **Sacral Chakra Detox:** You can perform a sacral chakra detox by drinking several glasses of water daily and eating fresh, organic fruits that contain a lot of water, like watermelon and pineapple. You can also eat fresh fruits like lemons and limes to enhance your metabolism. They are rich in water and contain vitamin C, which boosts your energy and strengthens your immunity.

These are just a few ways you can keep your sacral chakra healthy. Remember, your sacral chakra represents your relationship with the universe, and while it is vital for your well-being, it is also really important to balance your emotions and thoughts. You have to work at it to remain healthy — or else prepare to suffer from health problems such as depression, constipation, and lack of romantic relationships.

Chapter 8: Healing your Solar Plexus Chakra

The solar plexus chakra is about standing in your power and it relates to self-esteem, self-trust, and being rooted in your center.

This chakra helps to ground and center you. The focus of this chakra is on your power and identity. It governs your sense of self-worth and self-confidence. It is your center of purity, intentions, and the ability to take responsibility and accountability for yourself. If you are feeling disconnected from your power, it is very likely that your solar plexus chakra is blocked or in imbalance.

There is a significant connection between the solar plexus chakra and self-esteem. An imbalance in this energy center often triggers feelings of low self-worth and difficulty in getting in touch with your inner warrior fire.

Solar Plexus Chakra Meditation

Meditation for the solar plexus chakra can help relieve feelings of self-doubt and connect you with your self-confidence, sexuality, and sense of power. As the solar plexus chakra governs your self-esteem and sense of worth, this meditation is a wonderful way to connect with your center, ground yourself, and get inspired to stand up for yourself. And at the same time, this meditation takes a light, playful approach to learning self-love. Setting an intention for your chakra healing journey is a beautiful way to begin.

Remember that you are worthy of love. You deserve happiness and peace in your life. Stand up for yourself and for what matters to you. This meditation can be a wonderful tool to help you create the energy, relaxation, and healing that brings more balance to your solar plexus chakra and throughout the chakras. You can do this meditation anytime, anywhere, to feel more grounded, centered, inspired, and in tune with your body.

To connect with your solar plexus chakra, you can meditate and visualize by doing the following steps:

1. Find a comfortable seat or lie down in a comfortable position. Close your eyes and relax.

2. Take several deep breaths, connect with your body, and focus on the sense of grounding you feel in your feet.

3. Visualize this as a ball of yellow fire and feel it radiating through the solar plexus, the area above your navel, flowing down your spinal column, energizing your whole body.

4. Focus on the burning fire until you feel completely energized and alive. As you exhale, release any fears, pain, or expectations you may be holding in that area. Ask your solar plexus chakra what it needs right now.

5. Take several deep breaths and open your eyes.

Remember that the healing process needs your patience. Keep going until your journey is complete. Repeat the meditation every day as often as you can. Hold a golden flame in your hand and envision the color yellow as healing energy, or simply see a colored light buzzing around your solar plexus center. Chant when you're in the meditation phase, "I am a Warrior of Fire!"

Crystals and Stones for the Solar Plexus Chakra

Crystals help the solar plexus by absorbing and reflecting powerful energy. Therefore, crystals or stones can be beneficial to unblock and open blocked chakras and balance the energy flow in them.

Selenite: This stone is a wonderful stone to use on your solar plexus chakra when you feel that you are feeling anxious or overly emotional. Selenite is calming and soothing and can help bring your emotions back into balance. This stone encourages self-forgiveness and acceptance of yourself and others. Selenite is very safe to use in meditation as it does not retain energy.

Yellow citrine: Yellow citrine helps open your solar plexus chakra and helps relieve conflict, depression, and tension.

Lapis Lazuli: Lapis lazuli helps ease the conflict between yourself and those you love. It also helps you connect with yourself as it helps you express your feelings and bring self-expression into your life.

Red jasper: Red jasper can help balance the solar plexus chakra by neutralizing any negative energy you may want to release or let go of. It helps to release any tension and stress you may be holding and protects you from feeling vulnerable or out of control.

Amber: Amber balances the solar plexus chakra by soothing the stress you may feel when interacting with others. It helps stimulate connection with others as it encourages emotional expression.

Carnelian: Carnelian promotes a zest for living. It stimulates self-confidence and courage and helps regulate the inner fire of the solar plexus chakra.

Yellow aventurine: Yellow aventurine balances emotions so you can feel good about yourself again. It also aids in making wise decisions and helps you to take responsibility for your actions.

Yellow topaz: This stone helps you connect with your natural-born talents. It helps ease feelings of anxiety, nervousness, and unnecessary stress. It also encourages self-expression and creativity.

Turquoise: Turquoise connects the solar plexus chakra with attunement to hope and a healthy sense of self and others. It helps bring unity and balance into your life by stimulating self-healing abilities.

Chrysocolla: Chrysocolla brings self-confidence. It also boosts concentration and creativity. It helps clarify your thoughts and feelings. This essential oil also aligns with your desire to be your best.

Yellow agate: Yellow agate helps with fear of confrontation by helping you stand up for yourself. It also promotes inner healing and encourages self-expression.

Rutilated quartz: This crystal removes negative energy from your solar plexus chakra and energizes it with positive healing energy. It helps balance your emotions and stabilize your energy.

To work with these crystals, cleanse and charge them by smudging them with white sage, laying them out overnight under the moonlight, or using water. Get into a comfortable seated or lying position and hold your crystal in your left hand, the receiving hand, to receive the healing energy from the crystal. Allow your mind and energy to open to receive any feedback that may flow through.

You can also place a solar plexus chakra crystal two inches above your navel and take three slow and deep breaths. You may feel the energy of the crystal or slight static energy.

Yoga Poses for the Solar Plexus Chakra

Performing yoga poses can help the solar plexus chakra to balance and open when blocked. It promotes self-awareness as you become more aware of the feelings and emotions you are experiencing. Here are a few poses you can use:

- **Bird of Prey:** Begin lying on your stomach, bend your knees and bring the soles of your feet together, using your hands to lift your pelvis toward the ceiling gently. Stretch your arms high overhead. Hold for thirty seconds, then release and return to the mat.

- **Dreamweaver:** Come to lie face down on your mat, bend your knees and lift your feet off the floor, keeping your arms and legs straight. Hold for thirty seconds to one minute, then bring your heels down to the floor and rest.

- **Cat-Cow Pose:** Begin on all fours on your mat. As you breathe in, arch your back toward the ceiling and let your tailbone drop between your legs as far as possible. As you breathe, round your spine, tucking your chin in toward your chest and arching your spine toward the ceiling. Repeat this movement ten to twelve times.

- **Warrior II:** Stand with your feet spread about six inches apart and parallel, your toes pointed slightly outward, and your arms at your side. Make sure your knees do not go past your toes as you bend over and exhale as you extend your arm to the side, bending from your hips and extending through your fingertips. Keep your legs straight as you go between your hands. Bend from your hips to reach your left arm toward your right leg and let your right arm reach toward your left leg as you balance on one leg. Relax, lean forward, and take five deep breaths with one hand on either side of your head. Repeat on the other side.

- **Sun Salutation:** Begin in a standing position, inhale as you raise your arms overhead, exhale as you bend forward from your hips, and place your hands on the mat, slightly bending your knees as you inhale. As you exhale, return your arms overhead and bend forward from your hips again. Placing hands on the mat, bend your knees slightly as you inhale. Continue this breath pattern twelve times, inhaling to the upward-facing dog and three times exhaling to the downward-facing dog. Remember to breathe deeply and smoothly while moving.

- **Boat Pose:** Lie face down on your mat with your arms stretched overhead, hands interlaced with fingers pointing in the same direction, and legs extended behind you. Keeping your legs together, lift your arms and chest off the floor as you inhale. Hold for one or two breaths, lower your upper body to the floor as you exhale, and return to lying flat on your back. Repeat three to five times.

These yoga poses will open and uplift the solar plexus chakra. They teach you how to stretch and open the body by balancing the energy in this chakra to become more empowered and in touch with yourself. Breathing exercises like Breath of Fire and Bellows Breath are also effective.

Essential Oils

The solar plexus chakra upholds the principle of choice and balance. Essential oils balance your chakras by balancing your emotions and feelings. This chakra governs both our self-identity and our self-esteem. Essential oils help balance emotions such as anger, frustration, jealousy, greed, or fear, and these emotions often trigger feelings of low self-worth and unworthiness. Essential oils also support the process of self-forgiveness by releasing emotions such as guilt, shame, and blame.

A solar plexus chakra mix may include the following:

- **Lemon:** Lemon helps to relieve stress and tension that hold us back from expressing ourselves with confidence and courage.

- **Cedarwood:** Cedarwood helps support healthy self-esteem by helping you connect to your power. It can also help release negative emotions and stress.

- **Chamomile:** Chamomile supports healthy self-esteem and encourages self-forgiveness. It can also help calm and soothe feelings of anger, frustration, and anxiety.

- **Lavender:** Lavender promotes relaxation and helps calm your mind, body, and spirit. Sticks to your energy field and helps you feel safe in the world.

- **Roman chamomile:** Like chamomile, this oil supports self-forgiveness to help you let go of feelings of anger, guilt, and fear. It supports confidence and self-expression by reducing social anxiety and helping you connect more easily with others.

- **Grapefruit:** Grapefruit promotes healthy self-esteem and helps you be more confident. It can also help you release stress, tension, and frustration.

- **Orange:** Orange supports self-love and acceptance and allows you to act with courage and integrity.

- **Rosewood:** Rosewood helps you let go of negative energy and emotions to feel good and experience self-confidence.

- **Rosemary:** Rosemary helps to stimulate your power and helps center you when feeling confused and lost. It can also help clarify thought and can help bring clarity into decision-making.

Although any oil in your solar plexus chakra blend affects the chakra, these oils are particularly good for shifting your vibration to help you connect with your inner wisdom and strength.

Use a cotton ball to anoint your solar plexus chakra, or rub the oils between your palms to activate the chakra. You can also rub the essential oils a few inches above your navel area to open your solar plexus chakra.

Holistic Practices that Balance the Solar Plexus Chakra

Knowing that the solar plexus chakra is under constant attack from other people, self-care is the most effective method of keeping your energy balanced. When you feel hurt and confused by someone's actions, it is only a matter of time before you feel an imbalance in your solar plexus chakra. The best way to avoid this imbalance is to be self-aware of your inner truths.

Here are a few holistic practices that you can do for your solar plexus chakra:

- **Enroll and practice martial arts.** This method can help your solar plexus chakra feel balanced and open to being more aware of your life choices.

- **Connecting with nature.** Spending time in nature can help you connect to your inner wisdom in a relaxed environment.

- **Wear yellow clothing.** This step can help you stay empowered and happy.

- **Practice conscious breathing.** This step can also help you stay grounded and feel balanced in stressful situations.

- **Sleeping:** When the body is put to sleep or relaxed, the posture of the entire body changes. There are specific body positions for normal sleeping, which can improve our overall health.

- **Chanting.** The sound "RA" relates to the solar plexus chakra, which relates to courage, strength, will, confidence and fearlessness. Chanting "RA" for two minutes before bed can activate the solar plexus chakra, promoting better sleep.

- **Deep breathing.** Taking deep breaths when waking up activates our solar plexus chakra and provides sufficient oxygen to our entire body. Deep breathing can result in deeper sleep at night.

Chakras are energy centers that control the flow of energy throughout our bodies. You need to honor the chakras and work to center them again so that you can feel balanced, at peace, and capable of healing yourself, your loved ones, and the world.

Chapter 9: Healing your Heart Chakra

The heart chakra is about self-love, joy, and compassion. It is about feeling safe and loved. It is a place of compassion and love for yourself as you create a circle of safety around your energy body.

The heart chakra is located just above the heart area in the middle of the chest, down along the sternum bone. This physical center is interconnected with the rest of the chakras in our energy field. It contributes to your overall well-being by balancing emotions and providing a sense of calm and connection to those around you.

When our heart chakra is off-balance, we can feel disconnected and scattered because of our deep-rooted feelings of mistrust or fear of being hurt. This event can also lead to feeling stuck when there seems to be no way out.

Heart Chakra Meditation

Our chakra balances are foundational pieces in creating alignment and well-being in the physical, emotional, and spiritual aspects of ourselves. Take the time to be with yourself and sit with this balancing meditation that will help you if you find yourself in any of these situations. This meditation and visualization practice takes some time to cultivate, so be patient with yourself. If your heart rate is elevating, take a break and revisit when you're more rejuvenated. Here are some meditation steps for balancing your heart chakra:

1. Find a quiet place to close your eyes, whether sitting down or lying down.

2. Focus on feelings of compassion, love, and gentle strength to guide you through your meditation. Create a sense of safety around you, as if you are in a bubble of protection. Feel the stillness and let go of all anxious thoughts.

3. Focus on each heartbeat as you hold these feelings of love and compassion. Feel your chest expand with each beat and the warmth that fills your body as it beats with love. Then visualize a warm, loving light coming from your heart and then radiating out in all directions.

4. Visualize your heart chakra as a beautiful green light glowing in your chest's center. Focus on the color and how you radiate love and light with your heart chakra.

5. Continue as you focus on your breaths until you are calm.

Note: Creating a gratitude practice will also help you feel grounded, open your heart chakra, and send you more love and happiness. Take your time practicing meditation, and practice as often as possible. If you don't receive any intuitive hints, you may instead feel an awareness in your heart chakra.

Crystals and Stones for the Heart Chakra

Opening the heart chakra is about healing, accepting love from others, and understanding your self-worth. As we heal our hearts and open them to love, we also open ourselves to other truths and dimensions of existence. Then, you can have compassion and understanding for yourself and others.

Some crystals can help your heart chakra feel open and energized. They can enhance our physical, emotional, and spiritual growth. They can also help us with our healing and allow us to radiate our love and light. Here are a few of those crystals and stones:

Rose Quartz: Rose Quartz holds the energetic essence of love, compassion, and forgiveness. It connects your heart chakra with compassion, reducing stress and opening your heart to receiving love. It is a pink stone that helps with self-love and emotional healing. It helps to heal any feelings of emotional pain and separation.

Green Aventurine: Green Aventurine helps you feel safe in the world by allowing you to create that sense of protection around you, especially during meditation. It also helps your heart chakra become more loving and compassionate by reducing fear. A calm heart leads to better overall health.

Jade: Jade increases compassion and the capacity for kindness. As it helps you to be more open with your compassion, you restore balance to your heart chakra. This stone also helps you feel more protected and helps renew hope.

Turquoise: Turquoise connects you to the magic and mystery of the natural world, helping you open your heart to the universe around you while helping you stay grounded and focused. It releases stress and aids you in feeling more at ease and at peace.

Amethyst: Amethysts are purple crystals that help calm your overactive mind. They also help the pituitary gland balance hormones and reduce stress.

Emerald: Emerald is a green stone that helps your heart feel balanced and open to bring harmony to your life.

Lapis lazuli: Lapis lazuli helps you become open to love and to heal any past relationships and hurts. It is a blue stone that also helps calm an over-analytical mind.

Peridot: Peridot is a green stone that helps you feel more connected with your loved ones. It helps heal any feelings of loneliness and sadness.

Moonstone: This white stone helps your emotional body radiate warmth and calm.

To use these crystals, cleanse them by smudging them with white sage, lay them out overnight under the moonlight, then run water over them or soak them in salt water. Get into a comfortable seated or lying down position. Hold the crystal in your left hand or the receiving hand, and allow your mind and heart to open to feedback through images, colors, sounds, words, memories, emotions, or other impressions that may flow through.

You can also place your heart chakra crystal at the center of your chest and take three slow, deep breaths to activate the crystal or stone's power. You may feel the energy expand within your heart.

Yoga Poses for the Heart Chakra

Yoga poses can help the heart chakra feel balanced and open. These yoga poses activate our heart chakra through movement and help us connect with compassion, healing, love, and forgiveness. The following are a few yoga poses to help the heart chakra feel more balanced and open:

- **Runner's Pose:** Begin on all fours. Extend your arms in front of you. Stretch your toes back and point them up to the ceiling. Lift your knees off the ground and straighten your legs into a runner's pose. Once you feel stable, lift your hands above your head and hold one pose for about 30 seconds to one minute. Then release. Repeat three to five times.

- **Bridge Pose:** Lie on your back with your knees bent and feet flat on the floor. Place your hands on the floor. Straighten your arms and flex your feet. Press your thighs into the floor and try to straighten your thighs toward the sky. Hold this pose for 30 seconds. Keep your neck straight to reduce any strain on the back.

- **Bow Pose:** Stand with your feet together. Bend your knees and squat down, so you are on your hands and knees. Place your fingertips on the ground, spread your fingers wide, and lift your hips. If you want more of a challenge, lift your legs and roll over so that your back is on the floor and your legs are arched in the air. Hold this pose for a minute, and then return to a kneeling position.

- **Cow Pose:** Start standing with your feet wider than hip-width apart. Slowly bend your knees as you lean back, lowering yourself until your back is flat on the floor with your legs raised upward. Relax your arms in front of you as you keep your legs and back straight. Hold this pose for up to one minute, and let your breath guide you in and out through the nose only.

- **The Happy Baby Pose:** Sit on the floor or with your knees bent and feet flat on the floor. Place your hands on your thighs. Keep your hands rooted to the floor, sit tall with your shoulders back, and roll slightly forward. Relax your jaw as you breathe deeply for one minute.

- **The Bridge Pose:** Begin on all fours with your hands directly under your shoulders. Gradually walk your feet back while keeping your knees on the floor. Spread your fingers wide and keep your back straight. Hold this pose for about 30 seconds up to one minute, then slowly walk your feet forward to return to a kneeling position.

- **Eagle Pose:** Begin on all fours with your hands directly under your shoulders and your knees under your hips. Extend your legs in front of you and lift your hips, forming an upside-down V shape with your body. Walk your hands forward toward your toes. Hold this pose for about 30 seconds up to one minute, and then slowly walk your hands back to a kneeling position.

- **The Goddess Pose:** Begin in a sitting position with legs extended in front of you and feet firmly placed on the floor. Press deeply into your sit-bones and keep your back straight as you slowly lean back, letting your hands rest on the floor behind you. Hold this pose for one minute, then rest.

Essential Oils

Here are a few essential oils that can help your heart chakra become balanced:

- **Bergamot:** Bergamot oil calms your anxious mind while stimulating feelings of optimism. It helps regulate hormone production while releasing feelings of empathy and love.

- **Sandalwood:** Sandalwood is a calming oil that helps you feel more grounded and centered. It reduces stress and feelings of grief.

- **Rose:** Rose oil helps promote feelings of self-love and gentleness while also releasing emotional pain and feelings of loneliness.

- **Rose Geranium:** Rose Geranium oil reduces anxious feelings by calming your overactive mind and releasing feelings of stress.

- **Lemon Balm:** Lemon balm oil relieves emotional stress by refreshing your soul and mind while helping you feel free of fear.

- **St John's Wort:** St. John's Wort oil helps you become more open by stimulating your creativity and inner wisdom while calming anxious feelings.

To connect with your heart chakra, add a few drops of one of these essential oils to a larger portion of carrier oil. Apply right in the middle of your chest, or rub the oil between your palms to activate the properties.

Holistic Practices that Balance the Heart Chakra

The heart chakra governs your ability to empathize with others, love unconditionally, and feel compassion. It is your center of compassion, love, and forgiveness. To develop your feelings and connections with others, love yourself, and release emotional baggage and miscommunication, you must consistently balance your heart chakra. Here are some holistic practices that will help you balance the heart chakra:

- **Prayer:** Connecting to your spiritual self through prayer and meditation can help you feel more relaxed and open to others. Prayer and meditation can also help release emotional blockages so that you can experience feelings of love, forgiveness, and compassion.

- **Writing:** Before you go to bed or as soon as you wake up, write down at least one thing you are grateful for each day in a journal. This exercise helps you focus on the positive while opening your heart to feelings of love and gratitude. You can also record your dreams in your journal.

- **Sing:** Singing is a great way to feel your emotions while allowing your body and heart to release them through movement. You can try singing along to your favorite song or singing your favorite song on low volume while you work around the house to release your worries and stress for the day.

- **Work:** Volunteering at a local organization or animal shelter can help you feel connected to others and recognize your compassion for others in need. Find ways to give back so you can open your heart and become more compassionate with others. Volunteering can also give you physical benefits, such as reducing your risk of heart disease or high blood pressure while boosting your immune system.

- **Practicing forgiveness:** Releasing feelings of resentment and anger can help you open your heart to forgiveness. Practice forgiveness by releasing grudges and negative thoughts so your heart can remain open.

- **Massage:** Try a back massage, a gentle touch, or a foot massage to release tension in your heart chakra and help you feel more relaxed. Ask your massage therapist to use Deep Tissue Oil or Relaxing Massage Lotion to help release the tension that has become trapped in your heart chakra.

- **Chanting:** The sound "YUM" relates to your heart chakra, so try chanting as you inhale and exhale while focusing on your heart chakra.

- **Cleaning:** Give yourself a cleaning love bath at least once weekly to release pent-up negative emotions. A bath helps you release negative emotions and any lingering energy to help balance your heart chakra. You can clean your home to help balance your heart chakra, too. Cleaning your house can help clear the negative energy from your energy field and balance your heart chakra.

Keeping your heart chakra open is an important aspect of balancing your life. It can be easy to become overwhelmed by the difficulties in your life, but with holistic practices, you can balance your heart chakra and feel whole again.

Chapter 10: Healing Your Throat Chakra

The throat chakra is about expressing the truth and expressing yourself. It is about admitting when you have made a mistake and learning how to apologize and forgive yourself.

Unfortunately, as children, we are often taught to give away our power and hide our emotions. When we are hurt or upset, our parents protect us by telling us to "stop crying" or "not to make an issue out of it." As the years go by, we tend to do the same things to ourselves that were done to us by our parents, in that we shut down our throat chakra so as not to feel vulnerable or get hurt.

Addictions are often a result of suppressing our throat chakra and shutting down our ability to communicate. Use these techniques to open up to its wisdom.

Throat Chakra Meditation

Meditation can help the throat chakra to flow freely and open you up to the fullness of your emotions and your ability to speak your truth. We automatically think of the throat chakra as the center of our voice. However, it is much more involved in our communication than we realize. It is the center of our emotions and self-expression.

To connect with your throat chakra, do the following steps:

- Find a comfortable seat in a quiet room. Take a few deep breaths, inhaling through your nose and exhaling through your mouth.

- As you inhale, count to four; as you exhale, count to eight. This will focus your mind and allow you to observe your physical and emotional state.

- Feel the weight of your body in the chair, the air on your skin, and your legs. Focus your gaze upward with your eyes closed, twisting your head gently from side to side. Feel the weight of your head on the floor and your neck relaxed and open. Feel the warmth from your heart reflect into your throat chakra.

- Allow yourself to take a few mental notes about your body while you do this exercise. Breathe normally for a few minutes. Open your mouth slowly and bring your awareness to the vibration of your throat's sound when you swallow.

- Slowly add the sound of your voice merging with your throat's natural sound. Feel an open channel of communication form between the two sounds, like a flow of music through a flute. Also, notice any tension in your throat and throat chakra as you make these sounds. If this tension becomes uncomfortable, you can gently open your throat and experiment with different vowel sounds, asking your body what it needs to release.

- Continue this process for a few breaths, and then open your eyes as you return to reality.

Note: This meditation takes some time to practice, so be patient with yourself and take a break if you feel pain in your neck.

Crystals and Stones for the Throat Chakra

Crystals have healing properties and can help you balance your chakras. They are effective tools for personal development and meditation. Here are the best gemstones and crystals for the throat chakra:

Amethyst: This purple crystal is one of the most powerful stones to awaken and revitalize the throat chakra. It is useful for calming verbal confrontations and enhancing your clarity of speech. For power and strength, Amethyst combines well with Black Tourmaline, Rose Quartz, or Smoky Quartz.

Citrine: This chakra stone will help you clear your mind of verbal clutter and negative thoughts. Citrine brings positivity to your speech and is a powerful tool for healthy communication and expression.

Blue Chalcedony: This stone amplifies your energy, truth, and integrity. Chalcedony is the perfect stone to speak your truth while acknowledging your feelings and emotions.

Smoky Quartz: This beautiful gray stone helps open your throat chakra while clearing your mind of negativity. Smoky Quartz is one of the best stones for calming throat chakra imbalances and anxiety. Smoky Quartz also brings strength and stamina to your power.

Sodalite: This beautiful blue stone absorbs negative energy while revitalizing your throat chakra. Sodalite effectively expresses your truth while speaking your authentic self without creating harm.

Aquamarine: Aquamarine's power to awaken the throat chakra makes it one of the most useful stones for communication and harmonious relationships. This clear stone effectively strengthens your ability to communicate your feelings.

Fluorite: This stone brings structure to your communication and enhances your ability to express yourself thoughtfully. Fluorite is especially helpful for those who have speech difficulty as it helps you get rid of mental fog.

Black Tourmaline: This powerful stone helps you to speak your truth without anger or defensiveness and helps you to maintain your integrity in all of your communications. It is the best stone to protect from electromagnetic frequencies. Black Tourmaline heals your energy field while counteracting negative energies and vibrations.

Bloodstone: This stone helps you speak your truth, especially about your feelings, without anger or defensiveness. Bloodstone is an ideal stone for emotional mastery and soothing negative feelings.

Labradorite: Labradorite is a shamanic stone that can help you communicate with your spirit guides, bringing confidence and spiritual wisdom to your life.

Blue Lace Agate: Blue Lace Agate is a beautiful blue stone useful for stimulating the throat chakra. It encourages you to speak your truth to yourself and others and encourages you to trust yourself.

Howlite: This marbled white stone improves communication and creativity; used for public speaking, acting, and creative writing, since it encourages expression.

Lapis Lazuli: This blue stone promotes self-expression and inner peace, cleanses the energies of others, and sets your intention for using them.

You can clean your crystals by smudging them with white sage, laying them out overnight under the moonlight, or running water. To use the stone's healing qualities, get into a comfortable seated or lying down position and hold your chosen crystal in your left hand - the receiving hand - so you can receive the healing energy from the crystal. Ask the crystal to help you connect with the wisdom of your throat chakra.

Yoga Poses for the Throat Chakra

The throat chakra is about speaking your truth, so neck flexibility helps with fluency. Neck flexibility also helps improve blood circulation to the brain, which is an important communication component.

- **Bridge Pose:** The Bridge Pose stimulates the throat chakra while strengthening the back of the neck, shoulders, and back. It also calms the mind and helps you focus. To do the bridge pose, begin on your hands and knees. Place your knees hip-width apart, wrists directly under shoulders, and fingers slightly curled under. Tuck your toes under and lift your hips, coming into a neutral spinal position. Inhale and tuck your tailbone down as you lift your spine into an upward arch with the crown of your head reaching towards the sky. Place your hands flat on the ground for balance if necessary. Exhale and hinge at the hips as you tuck your chest towards your thighs. If you can keep your spine straight, clasp your hands and place them under your shoulders. On the inhale, lift your chest towards the sky, extending the crown of your head towards the sky 3-5 times. On the exhale, bring the chest back towards the thighs as you lower the head towards the floor, and then continue your practice of repeating this breath sequence a few more times until you feel your neck and upper back strengthening.

- **Camel Pose:** This pose stretches the upper back, shoulders, and back muscles, reducing stiffness in the neck and shoulders and alleviating numbness in the neck and throat. To perform this pose, sit on your heels on the floor with your heels and the back of your legs touching a wall. Hug your chin and hold your body back with your hands. Allow your head to fall towards the floor as you rest.

- **Cow Face Pose:** In the cow face pose, you sit cross-legged. Place your hands on your knees and sit up straight, inhaling while looking over the crown of your head at the ceiling. Exhale while gazing over your index fingers at the tip of your nose. Continue to breathe naturally for a few breath cycles while keeping your spine straight and your head upright. Inhale while arching your spine to look over the tips of your toes and exhale. This is a wonderful exercise you can do first thing in the morning. It opens your chest and improves your posture by stretching your intercostal muscles. It also improves your blood flow and breathing.

- **Shoulder Stand:** The Shoulder Stand is a deep body inversion that stimulates the heart and throat chakra. It improves circulation and releases tension and stress in the back and neck. To do the shoulder stand, first, place a folded blanket below the shoulder or cushion under your head. Hug the legs together behind you. Then, tuck the toes under and exhale as you press the hips up while lifting your tailbone towards the ceiling. Place your arms over the head and slowly lower the arms.

- **The Scorpion Pose:** This pose also improves blood circulation and alleviates tension in the shoulder and neck muscles. To do the Scorpion Pose, sit on the floor with your legs extended in front of you. Breast the floor with the bottom of your feet and your hands directly below your shoulders. Straighten your spine as you lift your chest towards the ceiling and gaze over your index fingers. Hold this pose for five breaths.

Essential Oils

Here are some essential oils that can help further your throat chakra healing:

- **Lavender:** Lavender oil is calming and relaxing to the body and spirit. Lavender oil is highly effective in alleviating stress-related physical problems such as fatigue, headaches, depression, and insomnia. It helps improve focus and relieves anxiety and depression by balancing your hormones.

- **Frankincense:** Frankincense oil is a blend of tree oils distilled from the resin of the tree Boswellia carteri. This oil has a scent that is very woody and sweet, reminding one of balsam and spice. Frankincense oil soothes and relieves stress, anxiety, and exhaustion.

- **Patchouli:** Patchouli is a herbaceous plant native to the Atlas Mountains of Morocco - sometimes called "liquid gold." Patchouli essential oil creates an earthy, spicy, and sweet fragrance. It is felt to be relaxing while still invigorating.

- **Ginger:** Ginger essential oil is warming, spicy, and slightly sweet. It stimulates circulation and relieves mental and physical fatigue. The healing energies of ginger oil are amplified when inhaled through the nostrils with a gentle face massage.

- **Rosemary:** Rosemary essential oil improves mental alertness and stimulates the mind. It enhances memory, concentration, and mental clarity. Rosemary essential oil is a strong antioxidant and antiviral and calms the nerves.

- **German chamomile:** German chamomile oil is herbaceous with earthy undertones. It promotes feelings of calmness and inner peace and also induces sleep. It may also help ease occasional stomach cramps and spasms in pregnant women.

- **Hyssop:** Hyssop essential oil is citrusy and herbaceous with floral undertones. Powerfully calming, hyssop essential oil sends healing energies to your circulatory system to help detoxify your body and stimulate the immune system.

Apply a few drops of any of these essential oils to a portion of carrier oil, and you can rub this mixture over your cervical spine to stimulate the throat chakra. A carrier oil is a vegetable oil that is used to dilute essential oils before they are applied to the skin. Carrier oils help to spread the essential oil over a larger area of the skin and can also help to reduce irritation and sensitivity to the essential oil. Some common carrier oils include sweet almond oil, jojoba oil, and coconut oil. You can also put a few drops of your chosen oil in a diffuser and breathe in this harmonizing aroma. To activate the throat chakra, say something like, "I now intend to create a connection with my throat chakra."

Holistic Practices that Balance the Throat Chakra

The Throat Chakra controls your ability to communicate thoughts, feelings, and ideas. When this chakra is balanced, you will have the ability to express yourself clearly and constructively. A balanced throat chakra helps you hear your inner voice and recognize your creative potential to feel good about who you are. When your throat chakra is imbalanced, you may feel incapable or unable to speak freely.

In addition to promoting good communication, the throat chakra controls the neck and shoulder muscles. You can incorporate many practices into your everyday life to help balance this chakra.

Here are a few other ways to open your throat chakra:

- **Chanting:** The sound chakra mantra for your throat chakra is "HAM". Chant "HAM" as a daily meditation to open your throat chakra for a few minutes.

- **Listening to Music:** Music that is energetic and can stimulate the movement of energy, like faster, louder music from a rock band or softer, soothing music from classical or country music, can directly affect the throat chakra.

- **Singing:** Singing your favorite music allows your voice to emerge unhindered.

- **Creating Art:** Create art that will express your inner feelings and include singing or speaking in a creative context.

- **Exercise:** Another powerful way to open the throat chakra is to exercise. Yoga, stretching exercises, spinning, dancing, running, and walking provide ways to work at opening this chakra to psychic and intuitive energy with its healthy flow of oxygen. Exercising is an excellent way to improve your voice if you have difficulty speaking in a certain situation.

- **Grounding:** To balance and open your root chakra, you can begin by learning how to ground your energy. Simply sit somewhere comfortable, close your eyes, relax your whole body, and breathe slowly and deeply for a few minutes. Place one hand on your heart center and the other on your belly. Close your eyes and breathe through your nose. As you breathe, imagine an energy flow going from your heart center to your belly center, down your legs, and into Mother Earth. Breathe for several seconds until your flow is firm and uninterrupted.

Balancing your throat chakra can positively change your life. It can make your dreams come true and improve your ability to speak and share your ideas with others. It can also help you develop more confidence by improving your ability to express yourself effectively and creatively.

Chapter 11: Healing Your Third Eye Chakra

The third eye chakra is about trusting your intuition and inner vision. It is often described as the gut feeling or sixth sense. All artistic work, including interior décor design, derives from this third eye, where creative energy finds expression. The royal indigo color is related to the third eye chakra. Make sure you are listening to your internal voice or guiding light, or you might miss out on some of the finer things in life, like the perfect job opportunity to improve your life.

You can activate the third eye chakra by drinking water and using an effective water purification system. You can also use the following steps and use these items to activate your third eye chakra.

Third Eye Chakra Meditation

The third eye chakra can highly benefit from meditation for its calming and centering effect. To practice, you can follow these steps:

1. Find a calm area within your home where you can sit comfortably. Then, close your eyes and try to clear your mind.

2. Visualize indigo-tinted light from within your skull and through the center of your forehead. Feel the light expand and fill your body.

3. Then start to breathe slowly and deeply as you see the light flowing endlessly from your third eye.

4. Just keep breathing in and out and relax your body and mind completely. Let your focus shift from your eyes to your third eye.

5. When you feel a sense of calm throughout your whole being, open your eyes after a few minutes and calmly end your meditation session.

You should practice this third-eye meditation daily to unblock your third eye chakra so you can be more receptive to new ideas and explore your creative side.

Crystals and Stones for your Third Eye Chakra

Healing stones enhance your connection with your inner vision and intuition. When your third eye chakra is balanced, the person can experience a spiritual awakening. These stones are primarily meant to give people wisdom and guidance regarding decision-making in their personal and career lives. If you are more stressed and overwhelmed because your third eye chakra is blocked, then you can use these objects to balance it.

Sapphire: This bright blue gemstone stimulates the pineal gland. It can help relieve stress and anxiety and can help you make the most out of your thoughts and intuition.

Lapis Lazuli: This blue stone is associated with the third eye chakra. It works great against emotional blockages and brings out inner strengths.

Citrine: This pale yellow gemstone can help people overcome negative thinking, which blocks their third eye chakra.

Peridot: This green gemstone can help manage negative thoughts and emotions and reduce insomnia.

Obsidian: This black stone can help detoxify the mind and body and remove negativity from your aura.

Pearl: This crystal is used for developing one's mental concentration and focus. It helps boost your third eye's clairvoyance. You can also wear your pearl in jewelry form to open your third eye chakra.

To work with crystals to connect with your third eye chakra, clean them by smudging them with white sage or palo santo, laying them out overnight under the moonlight, running water over them, or charging them with a selenite shard.

Get into a comfortable seated or lying down position, hold the crystal in your left hand, and ask it to help you connect with the wisdom of your third eye chakra. Allow your mind and heart to open to receive any feedback that may flow through. While lying down, place a third eye chakra crystal between your eyebrows and take three slow and deep breaths. You may feel a gentle heartbeat or slight static energy.

Yoga Poses for the Third Eye Chakra

Yoga can help you turn your attention inward and deal with any self-doubts and negativity holding you back from your goals and dreams.

When the third eye chakra is closed and out of balance, the mind and body become overstimulated and cannot do more than just react rather than respond.

- **Lizard Pose:** This pose, referred to as *Uttan Pristhasana* in Sanskrit, is good for activating the energy centers of your body. It benefits the third eye, the heart chakra, and the solar plexus. It also gives your brain the feeling of peace and calm, which can help you balance out your emotions. To perform this pose, begin kneeling on your mat in a tabletop pose. Then, step your right foot to the top of your mat outside your right hand. Walk your back leg back as comfortably as possible while your toes are tucked under. You can also lift your knee off the ground. Next, squeeze your feet toward each other to engage the hip and leg muscles. Reach your chest forward, keeping your spine long. Lower your forearms to the ground. You can place your hands on a block or a chair if the ground seems far away. You can hold this pose for a few breaths, then release it to the tabletop pose. Repeat on the other side.

- **Cat-Cow Pose:** This pose improves digestion and strengthens your back and abdominal muscles. It also helps you release negative emotions and stress as it moves energy through your body and balances your chakra centers. To perform this pose, start lying flat on your back with your knees bent so your feet fall away from your body. Make sure your spine is straight. Then, stretch your arms alongside your torso, keeping your elbows loose and pointed downward. Next, roll your entire body forward so your head goes back and your chest lifts upward. Repeat this movement five times up at the tip of the spine and five times down at the base of your tailbone. Reverse the movement, rolling your spine and neck back down and pointing your toes toward your feet.

- **Fish Pose:** Another yoga asana for the third eye chakra is *Matsyasana,* or the Fish Pose. It benefits your nervous system and also helps you build balance. It also gives you calm and peace and improves your circulation. To do this, lie on your back on the ground in the fetal position. You should bend your knees with your feet flat on the ground. Slowly curl your toes down, then curl your toes up. Repeat it ten times.

- **Bow Pose:** This pose is beneficial for awakening your chi and heart chakra. To do it, begin by sitting in the Lotus Pose. Next, bend your knees slightly and fold your feet under so that the soles of your feet touch each other. Hold your ankles with your hands and gently release them to the ground. Cross your arms over your thighs and sit comfortably with your spine straight. Lift your chest upward as you extend your arms overhead. Gaze at the floor between your arms. Hold this pose for five breaths.

- **Child's Pose:** To activate and open your third eye chakra, lie down on your back and bend your knees outward just enough to rest your feet on the ground. Rest your arms to the side, palms facing up, shoulders relaxed, and palms facing the ground. Close your eyes and take five deep breaths.

- **Headstand:** This position is designed to stimulate the opening and stimulation of the third eye chakra. Headstands help relieve back pain, heal the shoulders, balance the glandular and nervous systems, and relieve depression, insomnia, and anxiety. To practice, start by finding a wall with enough room to support your body while you are inverted. Use a block below your head and hands to help you balance. As you advance with this pose, you may want to use the assistance of a wall or railing to help you correct your form as you lean back or pull your head back slightly to take your weight off the hands and shoulders and onto the blocks below you. Once you feel comfortable balancing in this position, bring your forehead to your hands. Release your shoulders and chest away from your ears and roll your head back. Breathe normally in this position for five breaths, then exit the pose slowly and return to a seated upright position. Though the intensity of this pose can activate your third eye, it may not be for everyone, so be careful in trying this pose.

Essential Oils

Here are a few essential oils you can use for opening and helping unblock your throat chakra:

- **Geranium:** helps calm your mind and relieve anxiety and stress. It also helps open your third eye chakra.

- **Sandalwood:** This essential oil works to open your intuitive sense and calm your nerves.

- **Neroli:** helps boost self-confidence in your intuition and decision-making skills.

- **Rose:** This oil boosts self-worth and helps you feel more grounded.

- **Lemon:** This oil works to relieve anxiety and negative emotions, as well as eye issues and sinus illness.

- **Frankincense:** This oil is great for helping you focus your thoughts and open your mind to meditative states.

- **Vetiver:** This oil helps encourage you to follow your heart and intuition.

- **Eucalyptus:** This oil works wonders for relieving anger, stress, and negative thinking.

- **Grapefruit:** This essential oil is great for boosting positivity and releasing negative feelings of anxiety or anger.

You can apply a few drops of any of these oils to a small portion of carrier oil. To activate the third eye chakra, either anoint it or rub oils between your palms. Say something like, "I now intend to connect with my third eye chakra.

Holistic Practices that Balance the Third Eye Chakra

The third eye chakra is responsible for developing your intuition and helping you focus and concentrate. The following practices will help you gain a better sense of intuition through inner vision and will help you sharpen your ability to think creatively. Each practice can have profound benefits when done with intention and concentration, so do your best to focus on your mind, body, and emotions.

Holistic practices can help keep your third eye chakra balanced and open. Here are some of them:

- **Chanting:** To strengthen your intuition, chant the mantra "SHAM" repeatedly or "OM" for a minute daily.

- **Relaxation:** To open the third eye chakra, lie down and place your hands over your eyes as you concentrate on visualizing a light glowing between your hands. See the light shine outward from your hands and through your forehead in your mind's eye. Keep your mind's eye focused on the light for a few minutes a day. At the end of the session, place your hands on your heart, take a few deep breaths, and slowly open your eyes.

- **Journaling:** Keep a journal to help you follow the many signs and messages you receive from the Universe regarding your life path and decisions.

- **Breathing Techniques:** Practice deep breathing exercises to make you more aware of different rhythms and patterns in your life, body, and mind while increasing your spiritual awareness and consciousness. Practicing a few daily deep breathing exercises will help you feel calmer and more confident in your decisions.

- **Eating healthy:** Eating healthy foods and being physically active will help you stay grounded and focused. Try to balance your diet with the right amount of fats, carbs, proteins, vitamins, and minerals to support your higher energy levels and help you feel nourished.

- **Balancing exercise:** You can practice this exercise for an even stronger and more balanced third eye chakra. Simply lie down and make a circular drawing with your index finger along the inside curve of your eyebrow as you concentrate on your third eye chakra. Continue moving your fingers along your brow in a clockwise direction, then make a counterclockwise drawing near your hairline with your index fingers as you focus on opening your third eye chakra. Make the circle again and repeat this twice more for extra intensity.

- **Water release:** There are many situations in which we might feel stuck and not know how to move on, or we may not know how to express some emotions we have felt stuck facilitating. While taking a shower or bath, visualize all the negative energies shed and flow out of your body as you rinse.

Take caution when doing some of the following practices if you are pregnant or have trouble sleeping. Also, keep a journal handy, as you may have sudden and intense insights, dreams, and visions when you are in the flow of these holistic practices.

Chapter 12: Healing Your Crown Chakra

The crown chakra is about connecting with the Divine and our Inner Self. It is about opening to expanded spiritual consciousness. This energy center is about the connection to spirituality and the higher self. You can learn to connect with your own consciousness and with the universal consciousness.

We receive a direct link to the spiritual world through our crown chakra. Our crown center is where we connect with the divine, spirit guides, and ascended masters. In this chapter, you will learn a guided meditation that helps us connect to our higher consciousness and communicate with our angels and masters. This chapter also includes precious stones, yoga poses, essential oils, and other holistic practices to activate your crown chakra.

Crown Chakra Meditation

Meditation for the crown chakra can help you discover your true identity and connect to your inner divinity. This practice of meditation can unlock your full potential and awaken your sense of the profound spiritual experience of oneness. You will also learn how to channel the wisdom of the ascended masters, communicate with your spirit guides, and get one step closer to enlightenment. Here are the steps:

1. Find a quiet, meditative place to sit or lie down comfortably. Light a candle or dim the lights to create a peaceful atmosphere.

2. Close your eyes and take several deep breaths. Focus on your breathing. Inhale and exhale in silence. Focus on

the rising and falling of your abdomen as the lungs expand and contract.

3. As you breathe in and out, visualize white light moving in from the base of your spine to the crown. Visualize the light flowing through your body, going in and out of your lungs, going up and down your spine, rising into your forehead, and coming down.

4. Imagine that this light is swirling through your crown chakra. Feel the warmth of the light as it reaches the crown of your head, then let it flow freely in all the channels and chakras in your entire body.

5. Sit or lie quietly with the white light swirling in the crown center for around fifteen to twenty minutes. Concentrate on your breath as you relax. Allow yourself to be nurtured by the white light from your crown chakra. When your mind wanders, gently bring your mind back to the breath and visualize the light in the crown of your head.

6. Once you feel the energy wrap around your entire body, you can come back into consciousness and open your eyes.

You can repeat this practice as often as you like. Visualizations can help you focus on the crown chakra and connect with its energy. You can visualize the purple color radiating from your head's crown throughout your body. You can visualize well-dressed angels descending from heaven as you open your crown chakra.

Crystals and Stones for the Crown Chakra

Stones and crystals can benefit the crown chakra by charging it with positive energies and balancing the energy inside the chakra. Here is a list of crystals that are beneficial for the crown chakra:

Amethyst: Amethyst is a stone said to enhance spiritual awareness and wisdom. It can stimulate the crown chakra to open up to the divine spirit. It is said to promote wisdom, balance, and peace.

Aquamarine: Aquamarine is a stone said to promote empathy, compassion, and communication. The crown chakra is said to provide positive energy and awaken communication flows between the chakras. Aquamarine can help you open your mind to thoughts, feelings, and ideas.

Ametrine: Ametrine is a stone blend of amethyst and citrine, which both have beneficial effects on the crown chakra. It has strong metaphysical effects, helping you reach your potential and attain enlightenment and self-realization. Amethyst can help the crown chakra achieve wisdom and spiritual progress, while citrine is said to help you have good energy to achieve your goals.

Bloodstone: Bloodstone is used to balance the crown chakra and aid meditation. It is said to aid intuition and empower you to overcome challenges in life.

Opal: Cactus opal is a stone with tiny circles of quartz. It is said to positively affect the crown chakra, enhancing the flow of energies inside this energy center. It is also said to help you get in touch with your higher self.

Celestite: Celestite is a crystal said to calm the mind and connect you with the divine consciousness. It can open the way for communication with the higher self, spirit guides, and angels. It opens you up to spiritual experiences.

Clear Quartz: Crystal Quartz is said to improve the connection between the crown chakra and the rest of the chakras in our body. It is said to improve harmony within your mind and body and to heighten spiritual awareness and intuition.

Diamond: Diamonds are considered to be sacred stones, and they are believed to help you connect to your higher self. Diamonds can open the crown chakra to achieve self-realization, and they help you experience oneness with yourself.

Hematite: Hematite is an iron oxide with magnetic energy said to affect the aura and unlock creativity. Hematite is a powerful stone that helps the crown chakra clear auras of negativity.

Selenite: Selenite is a crystal used to manage energies. It enhances meditation and can help the crown chakra to channel the energies generated by the other chakras in the body. It is thought to be one of the stones connecting you with your higher consciousness.

To work with crystals to connect with your crown chakra, cleanse them by smudging them with white sage, laying them out overnight under the moonlight, or running water over them. To activate your crown chakra using crystals, get comfortable seated or lying down, hold your crystal in your left hand, and allow your mind and heart to open to feedback in the way of images, colors, sounds, words, memories, emotions, or other impressions that may flow through. You can also place your crystal at the top of your head and take three slow and deep breaths. You may feel a gently pulsing energy as you focus on it.

Yoga Poses for the Crown Chakra

The crown chakra symbolizes enlightenment, for it is the chakra between the physical and spiritual worlds. You can also refer to chakras as energy centers, which regulate the flow of information and energy between the physical body and the mind. It is the center of consciousness where we connect to our inner self and cosmic forces.

Practicing yoga asanas can clear your mind and relax your body to heal the crown chakra. It can channel energy through all other chakras in the body. The following poses can help you open the crown chakra and stimulate energy flow:

- **Mountain Pose:** The Mountain pose, also known as *Tadasana*, is a standing pose that helps your body and mind. It helps you achieve balance, focus, and focus. If you are a beginner, you can stand in one spot. Slowly bend your knees, lean back, and stretch your arms upward. The mountain pose helps you open the body, stretch your leg muscles, and increase the flexibility of your feet.

- **Warrior Pose:** The Warrior pose helps you increase vitality and energy. It strengthens and creates flexibility in the body. You can perform the warrior pose by standing straight with your feet together. You can bend your left leg backward and balance your body on your right leg. Hold this position for about 5-10 seconds, then switch your way through the position to your right leg. Try to balance yourself for a longer time on your right leg since you already hold a position on your left leg.

- **Headstands:** Headstands can help you gain balance and bring you in tune with your spirit. They are said to stimulate the crown chakra, lower your blood pressure, improve blood circulation to the brain, and stimulate your nervous system. You can stand on your head against a wall, couch, or bed. Place your hands on your head and slowly lift yourself while lifting your head from the hand. Make sure your legs are straight while resting on the wall, stool, or bed. Slowly lower yourself, and then repeat the exercise by standing back up. You can also practice a forearm headstand by resting your head on your hands, then resting your feet on the ground.

- **Shoulderstand:** The Shoulderstand posture, called the Sarvangasana in Sanskrit, stimulates blood circulation to the brain. The shoulderstand pose applies pressure on your shoulders and arms, helping to release stress from the body. You need to have enough space to stretch on the floor and lie sideways with your face upward. Try to balance your head on your stretched arms, resting your back on the floor. For beginners, you can place a pillow under your head to support and prevent you from resting on your palms. Hold this pose for a few minutes, and release it by slowly rolling down on your back.

- **Corpse Pose:** The Corpse Pose, the Savasana in Sanskrit, helps calm the mind and relax the body. To perform it, lie down on your back. Slide your hands under your neck so your body rests on your palms and elbows. Your face should be upward, and your eyes shut. Slowly lower your neck and head toward your torso. Hold this position for a few seconds, then slowly roll out to the sides and stretch your legs.

Note: Do the necessary stretching or warm-up exercises before performing yoga asanas. Immediately stop if you feel pain in your joints or muscles while doing yoga. The healing process takes time.

Essential Oils

Here are a few essential oils that you can use to balance your crown chakra and reach a higher level of consciousness:

- **Frankincense:** Frankincense is an oil extracted from the gum resin of the frankincense tree. It is said to help the crown chakra connect with your body and soul integration. It is also said to help channel energies from the upper chakras down through the lower chakras. Frankincense essential oil is burned or set in an aromatherapy diffuser to be smelled to help your crown chakra heal.

- **Lavender:** Lavender essential oil helps you relax and eliminate negative emotions, depression, and mental exhaustion. It is also known to help your crown chakra channel energy from the upper chakras down to all the chakras in the body.

- **Sandalwood:** Sandalwood essential oil helps you connect with your higher self and calm the mind. Incense Sandalwood helps you relax, calm your body, and connect with your higher consciousness.

- **Peppermint:** Peppermint oil is used to improve your mood, improve cognitive thinking, promote focus, and stimulate your body and mind. It also helps you release certain negative emotions when you use it with your crown chakra.

- **Lotus:** Lotus is another essential oil used to stimulate your crown chakra. Lotus oil helps you feel positive, centered, calm, and relaxed. It can also help you with meditation.

- **Rose:** Rose oil is used to relieve stress and anxiety and releases you from negative emotions. It aids you in achieving a higher state of consciousness.

- **Neroli:** Neroli oil helps you develop psychic abilities and get in touch with your inner self. It helps you connect with your inner self and helps you attain a higher state of consciousness.

- **Lemon:** Lemon oil helps you release stress, anxiety, and emotional pain. It is used to relieve tension and calm your mind.

To activate your crown chakra, apply a few drops of your chosen essential oil and a portion of carrier oil, then rub over your head and palms. Say something like, "I now intend to create a connection with my crown chakra." You can also inhale the fragrance by adding a few drops of any of the oils to a diffuser or a scented candle.

Holistic Practices that Balance the Crown Chakra

The crown chakra is the center for connection with your inner self and higher consciousness. This chakra helps balance the higher and lower chakras in the body.

- **Breathing:** Meditation helps balance the crown chakra, but breathing also helps you heal the crown chakra. Along with meditation, you can practice slow breathing exercises to balance the crown chakra.

- **Healing Touch:** Healing touch is a holistic technique that involves using your hands for energy. By touching the crown of the head or other parts of the body, you can heal energies in the chakra system. The crown chakra can heal very quickly since it is directly connected to the higher energies of the universe.

- **Grounding and Earthing:** The crown chakra is best healed by balancing the negative energies with positive energies. There are many ways to ground yourself by balancing your energies. Make sure you get yourself in a positive state by taking care of your daily mental, emotional, spiritual, and physical needs. Use salt and water while bathing to ground your body.

- **Tai Chi:** Practicing tai chi helps you feel calm and balanced. It releases stress, balances the energies in your body, and helps you interact with your higher self.

Healing the crown chakra is important as it is connected with our higher consciousness. It helps us get in touch with our higher emotions and intuition, let go of negative thoughts and feelings that stop us from connecting with our higher self, and helps us achieve a higher state of consciousness. You can heal your crown chakra rather quickly by using these holistic practices. Try them out and reach a higher state of consciousness in no time.

Chapter 13: Healing Multiple Chakras

Our chakras are connected on a web of energy flow, much like a river is a series of interconnected tributaries. When a chakra becomes out of balance – either energetically or physically – the energy from the other chakras can begin to affect and infuse itself into the chakra that has become unbalanced.

When working with your chakras, you want to keep them vibrant and in balance. Try performing the following activities a minimum of twice daily to help keep your chakras healthy and free-flowing. We are healthy, happy, and at peace when the flow moves freely. When the flow of energy is interrupted, so are its life-giving properties.

Meditation for Multiple Chakras

To start meditating for two or more chakras, do the following steps:

- Lay on your back and place one hand on each hip.

- Keeping the hips still and flat on the ground, relax your stomach and root down through the feet and legs.

- Slowly inhale through your nose as you turn your head down to one side. Let your head hang down without forcing or straining the neck muscles.

- Stretch your hands and breathe deeply. Hold your breath and pose for 2 to 3 minutes, then release by exhaling slowly through your mouth. Tilt your head back to the center, inhaling deeply, and repeat the pose to the other side.

This is a very easy activity, but one that most people do not do enough of. This practice only takes a few minutes a day, but the benefits can be very helpful.

Crystals and Stones for Multiple Chakras

You can energetically charge some stones and crystals to help balance multiple chakras. When you choose a stone or crystal to help energize and balance your chakras, find one that feels right.

For instance, some crystals have a strong vibration, or feel, of balance and harmony. They can therefore help to restore general balance and harmony, as well as support individual chakra needs. To do this, you can either wear the stone or place it on your chakras while meditating.

Some shops sell selenite wands that contain all seven chakra stones for overall chakra activation. You can also wear bracelets that contain two or more different stone types. Trust your intuition to guide you in choosing the right set of stones for your chakra healing.

Clear quartz is the most popular because it stores and transmits energy. Rose quartz is also an excellent stone because it is calming without suffocating and works to calm your emotions.

There are many different ways to use crystals to balance the chakras. You may want to experiment with ordering or purchasing different crystals to see which one works the quickest for you.

Yoga Poses for the Chakras

You can energize and activate your chakras by performing some yoga and breathwork exercises. Begin by doing the following yoga poses for each of your chakras:

Root Chakra: Tree Pose

Sacral Chakra: Goddess Pose

Solar Plexus Chakra: Boat Pose

Heart Chakra: Camel Pose

Throat Chakra: Supported Shoulderstand

Third Eye Chakra: Easy Pose

Crown Chakra: Corpse Pose

With practice, you can learn to gracefully align each of your chakras with the help of your hands, performing these cues in a flow of your design.

Conclusion

Learning to activate and balance the chakras takes time, patience, and courage. Once you know what to do and how balancing your chakras works, the process gets easier and more enjoyable. It is best to work with yourself regularly to realign your chakras. However, when you feel out of balance, remember the techniques and tips outlined in this article to easily restore energy flow to your chakras and start feeling better immediately.

Positive Affirmations - Part 1

Positive affirmations express the belief that a certain thing is possible. They can benefit anyone striving for a goal by teaching them to think positively. Some people read positive affirmations every day to achieve specific goals. You can benefit by repeating these simple statements to yourself to help you overcome negativity and succeed at your goals.

Repeating positive affirmations help you reach any goal you strive for by increasing your self-confidence, building a positive attitude, and boosting your determination. This helps you visualize your goal and realize the importance of reaching it. This can be any goal you have on your mind!

Now, relax and calm down as you repeat each affirmation five times in a row for two minutes each. You will listen to the affirmation, and there will be a pause of two minutes after each affirmation to give you enough time to repeat the affirmation and let your brain process it.

I am the most Powerful Being in this Body.
My seven chakras are in perfect alignment.
I have a strong and powerful connection to the Earth.
I am grounded and centered.
My chakras are spinning and rotating in a clockwise motion.
I am open to receiving all the guidance I desire.
I am open to receiving love, light, and healing energy.
I am willing to let go of all that no longer serves me.
I am ready to receive all the abundance that the universe has to offer.
I am full of love, light, and healing energy.

I allow myself to be vulnerable, knowing that I am safe and protected.
I am comfortable with myself and my chakras.
I am confident in my ability to heal myself.
I am inspired by the possibilities of chakra healing.
I use chakra healing to gain a deeper understanding of myself and my place in the world.
I am excited to explore chakra healing and to learn more about myself.
This is a beautiful world, and my chakras reflect the beauty of the world.
I am grateful for my chakras and the guidance they provide.
My chakras are a sacred experience, and I honor them as such.
I focus on having positive, beneficial experiences with my chakras.
I allow my chakras to reveal themselves to me.
I have full faith in my ability to heal myself.
I know that my chakras are a powerful tool that I can use to improve my life.
I am motivated and inspired by my chakras.
I am an infinite being of love and light.
I am safe.
I am protected.
I am Divinely guided and watched over.
I am abundant in all areas of my life.
I trust in the process of life.
All is well in my world.
I am worthy of love and respect.
I release anything that no longer serves me.
I forgive myself for any past mistakes.
I forgive those who have hurt me in the past.
I am open to receiving love, abundance, and joy into my life.
My heart is open and ready to receive love.
My mind is open to new possibilities.

My body is healthy, whole, and perfect.
I am surrounded by love and light.
The universe is conspiring to support me in all ways.
All my needs are met with ease and grace.
Doors are opening for me, and opportunities are coming my way.
I am in alignment with my highest good.
I know my worth, and I accept nothing less than I deserve.
I love and accept myself unconditionally.
I am kind and compassionate to myself.
I release all judgment of myself and others.
I embrace my imperfections as part of my perfection.
I am worthy of love, respect, and abundance.
I create healthy boundaries in all areas of my life.
I am free to be myself.
I am free to express my truth.
I am free to love and be loved.
I am free to create the life of my dreams.
My chakras are in alignment, and I flow with ease and grace.
My energy is cleared and balanced.
I allow my light to shine brightly in the world.
I share my gifts with the world.
I make a positive difference in the world.

Positive Affirmations - Part 2

The more I love myself, the more I can love others.
As I heal myself, I help heal the world.
I know that I am worthy of all good things.
I open myself up to receive all the good that life has to offer me.
I am blessed with an abundance of love, joy, and happiness.
I choose thoughts and experiences that make me feel good.
I am a magnet for positive people and experiences.
I am grateful for everything in my life, even the challenges.
I know that everything happens for a reason and that I am exactly where I need to be in this moment.
I surround myself with people who support, love, and respect me.
I take care of my mind, body, and soul.
I live life with intention and purpose.
I listen to my intuition and trust my gut instinct.
Everything I need is within me.
I activate and open my chakras easily and effortlessly.
I am open to receiving the full benefits of chakra healing.
I allow the energy of the universe to flow through me, cleansing and balancing my chakras.
I am safe and secure during chakra healing.
I release all fears and concerns about chakra healing.
I am open to experiencing all the benefits of chakra healing.
My chakras are in alignment, and I feel great.
My chakras are spinning rapidly, and I feel amazing.
I am confident in my ability to heal myself with chakra healing.
Chakra healing is a natural process that I easily and effortlessly participate in.

I am grateful for the infinite possibilities of healing that exist within me.

I have complete faith in myself and in my ability to heal through chakra healing.

Chakra healing is a sacred process, and I honor it as such.

Chakra healing is an important part of my self-care routine.

I make time for chakra healing every day, knowing that it is vital for my well-being.

Chakra healing is a fun and easy way for me to improve my life.

I am excited to heal myself with chakra healing.

I am open to all the possibilities of healing that exist within me.

The sky's the limit when it comes to my ability to heal through chakra healing.

I know that anything is possible with chakra healing.

I am worthy of love and deserving of healing.

I open myself up to receive the energy of the universe.

I am receptive to the healing energy that surrounds me.

I am surrounded by an abundance of love and light.

The universe is conspiring to heal me.

I am grateful for my body's ability to heal itself.

I am taking responsibility for my own health and wellbeing.

I am committed to my own healing journey.

Healing is a natural process that I trust and allow myself to experience.

I am open to all forms of healing, physical, mental, emotional, and spiritual.

I release all blocks to my own healing.

I am willing and able to do the work required for my own healing.

I have all the resources I need for my own healing.

I am supported in my healing journey by family, friends, and the universe.

My body knows how to heal itself, and I trust in its process.

Healing is possible for me, and I open myself up to it now.
I reject anything that does not support my highest good.
My intention is to heal myself in mind, body, and spirit.
To support my healing journey, I make healthy choices in thoughts, words, emotions, and actions.
Everyday I take actions that are in alignment with my highest good.
I give myself permission to heal.
I am worthy of healing.
I accept myself exactly as I am.
I am entitled to heal.
I am committed to my own healing.
My intention is to be healed in mind, body, and spirit.

Guided Meditation

Begin by lying down, letting yourself get comfortable, ideally flat on your back with your spine straight, legs uncrossed, arms at your side, palms facing open, however, if that is not comfortable for you, make comfort your priority and when you're ready, lovingly close your eyes.

Invite your awareness in words.
Tuning into your own inner landscape.
Feeling your breath.
Inviting it to flow as softly and naturally as it wishes.
Relaxing and allowing gravity to take over.
It's safe to let go.
To release into relaxation.
Now think about your intention for this practice.
Why do you want to heal your chakras?
What is it that you hope to achieve?
Allow yourself to really feel into your intention.
And as you do, begin to see a bright white light in front of you.
This light is cleansing and healing.
And it begins to move into your body, entering in through the crown of your head.
And as it does, you may feel a sense of relaxation and peace.
This light moves down through your body, cleansing and healing as it goes.
You may feel a sense of warmth, or of tingling, as it moves.
Allow yourself to simply relax and receive the healing that this light is offering.
And as it moves down through your body, it enters into your heart.
And you may feel a sense of love and forgiveness.
Allow yourself to simply relax and receive the healing that this light is offering.

And as it moves down through your body, it enters into your solar plexus.

And you may feel a sense of power and confidence.

Allow yourself to simply relax and receive the healing that this light is offering.

And as it moves down through your body, it enters into your sacral chakra.

And you may feel a sense of creativity and pleasure.

Allow yourself to simply relax and receive the healing that this light is offering.

And as it moves down through your body, it enters into your root chakra.

And you may feel a sense of stability and security.

Allow yourself to simply relax and receive the healing that this light is offering.

And as it moves down through your body, it exits out through the soles of your feet.

And you may feel a sense of grounding and connection.

Allow yourself to simply relax and receive the healing that this light is offering.

And as the light exits your body, it moves back up in front of you.

And as you look at it, you may see any colors that you wish to see.

And you may feel a sense of peace and calm.

And when you are ready, very slowly roll your shoulders, and wiggle your fingers and your toes.

And only when you're ready.

Take your time as you open your eyes back to the world around you.

Thank you, namaste.

MELISSA GOMES

FREEBIES

AND

RELATED PRODUCTS

WORKBOOKS
AUDIOBOOKS
FREE BOOKS
REVIEW COPIES

HERE

HTTPS://SMARTPA.GE/MELISSAGOMES

Freebies!

I have a **special treat for you**! You can access exclusive bonuses I created specifically for my readers at the following link! The link will redirect you to a webpage containing all my books and bonuses for each book. Just select the book you have purchased and check the bonuses!

>> https://smartpa.ge/MelissaGomes<<

OR scan the QR Code with your phone's camera

Bonus 1: Free Workbook - Value 12.95$

This **workbook** will guide you with **specific questions** and give you all the space you need to write down the answers. Taking time for **self-reflection** is extremely valuable, especially when looking to develop new skills and **learn** new concepts. I highly suggest you *grab this complimentary workbook for yourself*, as it will help you gain clarity on your goals. Some authors like to sell the workbook, but I think giving it away for free is the perfect way to say **"thank you" to my readers**.

Bonus 2: Free Book - Value 12.95$

Grab a **free short book** with **22+ Techniques for Meditation**. The book will introduce you to a range of meditation practices you can use to help you develop your inner awareness, inner calm, and overall sense of well-being. You will also learn how to begin a meditation practice that works for you regardless of your schedule. These meditation techniques work for everyone, regardless of age or fitness level. Check it out at the link below!

Bonus 3: Free audiobook - Value 14.95$

If you love listening to audiobooks on the go or would enjoy a narration as you read along, I have great news for you. You can download the audiobook version of *my books* for **FREE** just by signing up for a FREE trial! You can find the audio versions of my books (depending on availability) at the following link.

Join my Review Team!

Are you an avid reader looking to have more insights into spirituality? Do you want to get free books in exchange for an honest review? You can do so by joining my Review Team! You will get priority access to my books before they are released. You only need to follow me on Booksprout, and you will get notified every time a new Review Copy is available for my latest release!

For all the Freebies, visit the following link:

>> https://smartpa.ge/MelissaGomes<<

OR scan the QR Code with your phone's camera

I'm here because of you

When you're supporting an independent author,
you're supporting a dream. Please leave
an honest review by scanning
the QR code below and clicking on the "Leave a
Review" Button.

https://smartpa.ge/MelissaGomes

Made in the USA
Las Vegas, NV
28 July 2023

75337661R00089